TRAINING FOR PLACEMENTS

RAJENDRA CHANDORKAR

This book

is

a tribute

to all those working in

the Training for Placement Departments

Contents

Preface *vii*
Acknowledgements *xi*
1. The Present Scenario 1
2. Sector Analysis 9
3. Training For Placements Idea And Concept 16
4. The Tpo And His Work Cut-out 25
5. Expectations Management 35
6. Stakeholders And Their Perspectives 40
7. Role Of A Trainer In The Process Of Placements. 46
8. Final Semester Pangs. 55
9. Mentoring In Training For Placements 63
10. Role Of Microsoft Excel In Placements. 71
11. Proposed Placement Process 74
12. Skill Development (local & Global) 79
13. Jobs In The Future 94
14. The Actual Process 100
15. The Digitalisation (the World At The Fingertips) 125
Conclusion 131

Preface

PREFACE

Training for placements is an effort to change the paradigm from the current phrase used in almost all colleges which is "Training and Placement." While working as a trainer, I understood the need for specific content for the training required for the placement. The correct elimination of the matter not needed was very important for me. When a lean and trim content was developed over some time, I could do a better job on the assignment. The students are as it is overloaded by a lot of avoidable stuff. It is felt that there is a need to rethink and rephrase "Training **for** Placement."

The training and the placement effort has to be a very well-balanced activity and needs constant finetuning by the TPO. The biggest folly that is adopted by the colleges is to appoint separate heads for both activities. There is a congenital defect in such an arrangement, wherein each would blame the other. Students suffer very badly and tend to avoid both.

The TPO would be very wise in knowing the limited vision of the stakeholders and he would further be needed to perform. He would follow the three basic rules. The first is to perform with available resources, the second is to accept the students strictly on *as is where is* basis, and the thirdly involves the students in the process.

The T&P as it is called presently is more talk than action. A lot of people do a lot of things and yet when the desired results are not obtained a big run from the issues race begins.

The student-specific training is rarely designed and generalized training is provided in a very ordinary fashion. The question which is the first thing the trainer has to answer is never even looked into. 'Why should I listen to you?' is the question that is never satisfactorily answered. The students attend the sessions with minimal interest and the result is very poor.

The trainer has to be a dedicated variety preferably on the payroll of the college and not fashionably outsourced. There is a specific reason. Barring a few honorable exceptions, the resourced persons care more for their reputation. They use these opportunities as self-promotion programs and deliver a lot of unnecessary and confusing material to an already confused bunch of students. It is seriously suggested that each respectable college must have its own in-house and capable training department, where accountability can be fixed.

Many colleges carry out fashionable training festivals, and camps, inciting all those coterie people who have no interest in the training or betterment of the students. The students confide in us the ranked outsiders and tell a lot of stories about the caliber of the visiting persons. The training sessions should be in the interest of the. students and not for the obligatory fulfillment of the UGC or NAC regulations. The students should decide what they want and how they want to proceed, of course, in consultation with the TPO. Again, the practice of a political appointee for the Dean or Head of the T&P Department must be discarded. This person so appointed uses this as a reason for not engaging in the teaching classes, and does not, as a rule, contribute to the T&P activity because he has no inkling of the activity. He is generally a speed breaker than a catalyst. One thing similar to a catalyst he does is that he comes out of the process unaffected. One more aspect of the entire T&P activity that has to be looked into is whether a Ph.D. is at all required. All reasonable people would tell you that the T&P department must directly report to the chairman of the college if any worthwhile results are to be achieved.

T&P is not an OJT activity. Some worthwhile previous experience in the industry, marketing, negotiating, and communication is a must. Even if the teachers had earlier worked in the industry very rarely, they fit the bill. The ego systems of the teaching and training streams are totally different and very rarely understood by the principal as he is also from the same production unit. If extended the same is true for the vice-chancellors and the chairmen of UGC etc. once and for all it should be accepted that T&P is a hardcore sales activity and a person from core sales activity should be appointed and then given a free hand to operate.

The selection of faculty coordinators, from various departments, is another aspect that the chairman of each college must look into personally. The qualifications do not matter as much as the aptitude and the interest of the students. One day, spent here by the top management, minus the academics, can bring at least twenty-five percent more quality placements. The direct involvement of the chairman resolves a lot of unpleasant and conflict of interest issues.

One more issue that the chairman must look into, is, to just plainly remove all those teachers, who complain about the input quality of students. The input quality is as per the parameters of the admission process. This statement is the biggest dampener on the entire T&P process. This would regularize a lot of processes. Again, the exceptions would be there.

Issues trainers must always remember:

1. Dealing with mature students. Instead of complaining that the students are not receiving or responding the trainer must be able to use their limited response and then convert it for their benefit. It is very difficult to mold a student who is already learned a lot of unwanted things. The trick lies in the art of getting the board cleaned and a new set of instructions to be imbibed into the minds of the students who need to change and change quickly. It is difficult, highly improbable but he must remember that it is not IMPOSSIBLE.
2. He has to ensure that they are in listening mode. Generally, they are not. We cannot blame them for this state of mind. They have seen and heard a lot of unwanted, demotivating stuff in their stint at the college. A demonstration of an inverted pot and water jug generally conveys the point.
3. Nothing is automatic: Henceforth, in the lives of the students seeking a placement, nothing would be automatic as it was so far in their lives. stressing this point clarifies that if they do not do what is required of them, they are in for doom very soon. Stress it further on their minds that they either do it now or later in a worse scenario. The choice is theirs and collateral damage also.
4. Training is boring: Accept it. Also, tell them that you are not responsible for the same. You are a trainer, not a standup comedian. You are not there to entertain but to train for a serious issue like getting properly placed. Never fall for the make it interesting trap thrown by outsiders. You can do the following exercise with the students. Ask them what they like to do. They would name outings, movies, dating, riding, long drives, and restaurants or many others. Accept and put in the next question. Where do you get money from? Some mischief mongers would say that their parents give them. Where do they get the money? By doing **boring jobs** in banks, offices, etc. To conclude you can say that all interesting things need money which is earned by doing boring jobs, and training sessions at the beginning of getting bored to do interesting things in the future.
5. You can tell stories: Yes, stories can form a very great stress buster or a light diversion. But that must never be at the cost of the content you are supposed to deliver.
6. Get a command: Get a commandand then never lose the same. Casual

dominance is a term the trainer should never forget. Once the students feel that they are with the right person they deliver fantastic results.

7. Let the students: The students have a wonderful knack for participating and they love to control and deliver. As a rule, the trainer must never evaluate the activities like GD or PI but he should allocate the participants to do the same.

The people in T&P would get a feeling that they have done something great when the students get placed. There is a temptation of playing God. Stay away from such stupid things, on the contrary thank God that he has chosen you as a medium to make people happy.

***

Acknowledgements

Acknowledgments

During my stint in the Training For Placements activity, I was helped by many angels and friends. They discussed, taught, corrected, and most importantly, they behaved like normal human beings. They were the difference that helped me to distinguish during the dreadful atmosphere. I acknowledge their help.

The students helped me to know the deep water details. What they shared with me about their teachers, management and peers helped me hugely in formulating a worthwhile strategy for a steady number of placements. They accepted me after a while and they told me later on that they were pleasantly surprised by my approach. I would have never been successful without their implicit faith in me. The student coordination committees in each department of the colleges went way beyond their scope and produced fantastic results. I could see a remarkable difference in their attitudes when they started working on the committees.

The companies, the other part of the Placements process was equally responsible for enlightening me about what they want and how they want me to train my students to be more employable. Infosys, Accenture, TCS, Tech Mahindra, HSBC bank, Patni Computers, Asian Paints, Naukri.com. Monster.com, Cocubes, Afcons, Shapoorji Pallonji, and so many others actually cleared many dark areas. I acknowledge their help with all gratitude.

The management for whom I worked had some of the best in the fields of training and administration. They guided me with their light-hearted one-liners when I needed the push and encouragement. When I compared my lots with the people from other colleges I could thankfully see the difference and hence I wholeheartedly appreciate and acknowledge the help and financial clearances needed.

Rajendra Chandorkar.

CHAPTER I

The Present Scenario

The Present Scenario

The entire activity of job placements for students passing out of the professional and degree colleges is new in India. Earlier, the colleges were few, which could be counted on the fingers, and correspondingly the number of students was also relatively low, students would be somehow placed. The expectations of the students were reasonable, the lifestyles were easy, so the graduate pass-outs were generally absorbed in the nearby government departments or industries. Once employed, he would work for his lifetime and *retire* from the same office or at worst from a branch somewhere in the region. He was satisfied, as was his wife, and kids. Their expectations were low. The cost of living was low. If you feel so, you may run a check on the prices of gold and petrol in the early sixties, seventies, and even in the eighties. You would be shocked. Something seriously went wrong, in the later years of the seventies. It was a delayed effect of acts of many inefficient leaders along with their major follies, wrong policies, emotional decisions, and very wrong implementation of the lopsided educational policies. The changes in the policy were not because they were needed, but due to the whims and fancies of the so-called visionaries who later proved to be myopic. They were more concerned with their religion, and castes. The basic ingredient for any worthwhile and long-lasting national policy is rational thinking and logic behind the same. If one is curious enough and decides to trace the education policy, he would be surprised that there was *nothing like* the **national education policy** till a very long time after independence.

The replacements of the policies which were working for centuries worked totally against the basic principles of education. The people who induced the changes were neither competent nor inclined rightly. Very few were interested in the welfare of the students, or the history, or even in the lessons from our history. Some were intoxicated by the policy of downplaying the traditional Indian wisdom, later on, it all combined to deteriorate the once very strong education principles in ancient Bharat. The unnecessary impact of people who should never have been in educational policy-making was simply devastating and long-lasting.

The first authentic Education Policy came into existence in 1968, developed by Kothari Commission. This was after 21 years of getting independence. This itself shows the priority of the then-ruling party. Subsequently, the paper called policy was released in 1986,1992 and 2020. It is also to be noted that the 1986 policy, which was launched as *the ultimate* was refurbished in 1992. So, in short, there are three versions of education policies. Their contribution, to the improvement of Indian education, is a matter of serious debate and research. The basic reason for any policy is to improve the existing one for the betterment. Can you say so about our education and the caliber of the students? Now, it is felt that instead of just doing some change here and there, someone more sensible, capable, and willing must put in an intensive and comprehensive effort to create something worthwhile.

The guiding principle was to erase the ancient culture and the guiding Sanatan principles which were good to last for centuries in the past. The modernIndian way of making policies always overlooked capable, sincere, and conscientious people. They were replaced by the inefficient, undeserving, and *coterie* types who further destroyed what could not be earlier destroyed by the people like McCauley.

The effect started to become visible in the early eighties. The issue needs some deliberation on a serious note. **The separation of knowledge from the degree** was evident. Earlier, even a third-division BA could write and read in a much better way than its later-dated version. The lowest point came to the fore when postgraduate students started applying for a post of a peon in government departments and failed. People started writing articles in a lighter vein, when in actual practice, they should have seriously condemned and used their wits, as well as intelligence, in finding out suitable solutions for the improvement of the system.

The decay in education is a result of a gradual decline in the a) quality of teachers, b) their corrupt recruitments, c) their attitudes, d) immoral practices rampant in the sector, and so many such things. In India, a serious folly called a <u>compromise with caliber</u> was adopted by the politicians because it suited them. The quality of the leaders, administrators, and top policymakers was always in a doubt. If the quality was good then the integrity was questionable. If it is not true then it should reflect in the quality of the students.

Many leaders **jumped** into the education sector, not because of their love for the students or education, but for the simple reason of almost free land, a stable flow of money in the form of capitation fees, and an unquestioned authority over the teachers. The conditions of teachers in such institutions are worse than the bonded labor in the earlier system of farming and coal mines.

The management in such institutions was a demonstration of how money and political power can dominate people with caliber. The teachers and the students were the last priority and **revenue was the only** and main issue. All the stakeholders, barring a few genuine institutions, had no interest or inclination for the betterment of the education or the students. Everything could be *managed* and sadly for the nation, it was done so. They could never understand that **education and revenue** are two different things and they can **never mix**. Maybe for a while, the mixture can appear like a homogeneous solution, but it never stands the test of time. When everything was concerned with the money inflow, corruption could not be far behind. The manipulation of the a) attendance of students, b) allowing mass copying, c) the marks in the internal exams, d) the oblique way of managing the evaluation and the evaluators somehow could run the show for a while, but in the final run, it was a certain rush to ruining the name, fame and the inflow of the students and the institutions. Now the closures of the departments and even colleges bear a true and dark testimony of the wrong policies of the government and the management.

In a candid one-to-one and off-the-record discussion, a chairman of a renowned educational group was asked to name five teachers in his empire who were magnetic enough to pull the students. He admitted that the quality of his teaching staff was (and even today it is the same) not up to mark. He confessed that very few of the teaching staff could use English, the language of instruction as a medium to teach fluently for the duration of the lecture. He also confessed that most Ph.D.'s and professors never engaged in the lectures and their Academic Load was delivered by the lowly paid immature and temporary teachers. That the principal or the director of the institution is supposed to take some mandatory number of teaching sessions is a big joke and such a person is as rare as a black pearl.

The basic requirements for the teachers are not fulfilled.

The teachers were paid low, irregularly, once in three or four months and yet they were supposed to teach the students who were below par. *One line summing up the trend can be all educational institutions were minus education.* The focus was never on education, delivery of knowledge, research, or improvement of the students, and so that shows in the lack of quality of students. The lack of seriousness on the part of management and teachers finally rubs on the students who become disinterested.

The students are blamed for the fall in the standards of higher education, which is as rubbish as the garbage. **No student is bad! No student takes admission to college to fail or to perform below par.** Moreover, he has generally met the basic admission criteria required for the curriculum like engineering, management, medicine, law, and many such options. Once accepted the teachers or the management have no right to *criticize the input quality.* When the same students paid the hefty fees, everybody was happy. The student then approached the campus, with all its fulfilled and unfulfilled promises, he was even *then* very optimistic about his future. After all, the *admission mafia* promised him so much. The glow in the eyes of the students in the first semester of engineering or MBA is there to be seen. They are looking up to the teacher as a perfect person to make them adequate engineers or managers. The glow is doused by the sad attitude of the teachers. The a) disinterest in teaching as their profession, b) their mechanical delivery, c) the same jokes repeated for decades, d) the terrible pessimism, killed the students mentally year after year. Due to an inbuilt frustration developed due to various reasons, over a period of years, a major section of the teachers takes out a fiery ire on the students. The poor students never know why they are fired left right and center by the teachers. The threats are rampant and very wild. The entry of teachers into the teaching field is generally their last resort. Very few post-graduates want to be teachers. One thing they conveniently forget is that the ***student is not responsible*** for a) their failures, b) their less salary, c) their continuous exploitation, d) the failed government policy, e) unfurnished labs, f) insufficient library, g) poor facility in the faculty room, h) disrespect from the management and many such things. So, when a teacher enters the classroom and starts his discourse of topics, he must ideally forget the outside world and concentrate only on teaching. If he cannot do this simple thing he should just get out of college and search for something else as a career.

In our ancient culture, where Sarasvati, the goddess of knowledge is at the top and treated as superior to Laxmi, the goddess of wealth, was long forgotten and the only thing that mattered was money and more money. Money in any which way possible! The owners had money, they had political power, and they had people in the right places so they could manipulate the results at least on paper.

The word FACULTY is a word used very loosely, just like the title professor. A teacher has to evolve into a professor over a long period. It is a hard and tedious journey.

FACULTY is a word that needs some serious introspection. It has a c as a core. The C stands for:

- The core of the subject
- caliber
- concern
- care
- content
- concise
- correct input
- consistency
- capable to deliver correctly
- communication

There can be a few more but it does not matter. What matters is that the faculty must understand that he takes out C from the word faculty what remains is FAULTY.

A disinterested and demotivated teacher has no right to be on campus. He is spoiling generations and nations. Such teachers are worse than serial killers. The entire process of education is good or bad because of the teachers.

So, to become a good and sought-after teacher, the faculty must think and deliberate about the following points:

- Preparation
- Presentation
- PowerPoint dependent
- Effect of voice on teaching
- No idea about voice modulation
- Preferences
- Professional ethics
- Prejudices
- Patience
- Pay package
- Paid coaching / extra money

- Lack of practice
- Lack of patience
- Lack of integrity
- Age-old and yellow notes
- Lack of humor
- Lack of updating of knowledge
- The teacher has to be an actor
- Unnecessary criticism
- Practice what he preaches
- No understanding between a teacher and a Guru.

One of the most sickening things that have struck the junior colleges in our nation is a hand in hand collusion operations by the private tuition classes spread across the nation and they have taken over the weak or wicked management of the educational institutes. In the last decade or so, these coaching institutes have spread like a wildfire. The admission to *the number one* coaching class is more of an occasion to celebrate, than the result of the tenth standard. Check up in any home where a student has passed the SSC exam and you would be surprised. The fees are astronomical (on an average of Rs. three to six lacs for the two years duration) and they are in addition to what the parents pay to the college. The fees paid to the college are a *total waste* as the classes for the eleventh and twelfth standards are never engaged. Again, there would be some exceptions but they merely prove the rule.

The students who are not ready to attend college, somehow attend the coaching classes, with the bare minimum or no facilities. The admission clerk at the coaching center decides the admission of the student to college. The way they talk about the college in question tells you that the college is in complete control of the nexus. All the educational qualifications like Ph.Ds.', the experience of the teachers, the infrastructure of the college, and the reputation of the college simply lie in the feet of the *uneducated* clerk seating there and making a complete mockery of the system.

The proof of the pudding is in eating. Whatever the inputs, and methods of cooking and baking, if they do not end up in a tasty pudding, they are an exercise in waste. Similarly, whatever the students do, whatever the colleges claim about the quality of their students, their five-star infrastructure, and the placement records, all you need is one interaction with the students in the engineering and MBA is enough to know that things are not right.

Whenever any problem is reported, the first reaction is denial. If the whistle-blower is persistent, he is taken to the chairman and permanently silenced.

If there is any repair or corrective action taken, it just adds a few more excel sheets, circulars, and sessions by someone close to the management. The logging is perfect, and the photographs are even more perfect but it yields *nothing worthwhile.*

On such background when we discuss the training for the students, the management is not interested in proper training set up, as for them it is an additional expense. There are a lot of lobbies, *'you scratch my back I scratch your'* groups, who are engaged in such activities, but rarely produce any results.

That education is *not only the exams* and *passing with good marks,* was long forgotten in the initial years of Indian independence and that lapse still haunts the education process. The inculcation of *national pride and national spirit* is missing. The way the national songs and anthems are recited in educational institutions is a shame. It is mechanical without any feelings. Further, there are no uniform rules. What is practiced in the missionary schools and the madrasa schools is well beyond any control. While most Indians are working for the betterment of Indian ethos these people seem to have some separate agenda. The perception management in these aspects of education needs a review.

Most of the education is handled by callous people who earned money by all corrupt means, they do not see education as a significant factor in the success of an Indian. Sadly, if you consider money as the sole and important factor then you are very right. In India, you do not need to have *education or even literacy,* to earn money and power. Check the background of most leaders and you would be surprised. They manipulated their education, and they flaunt their rustic attributes very shamelessly. In fact, in Indian movies, the teachers are treated in a listless fashion, with complete humiliation. The selection of teachers, the recruitment, their postings, their transfers, the sexual exploitation of female teachers, and the inefficient teachers spoiling generations of students continue in a very dirty way. Respect for the teachers is non-existent. Again, there are welcome exceptions, but they are as rare as a black pearl.

If you feel like, you should talk to any student, question him and you would have a detailed perspective on the ground reality. The best thing about placements of students is **everyone knows what is to be done,**

especially others and then he waits for things to fall into place.

CHAPTER II

SECTOR ANALYSIS

SECTOR ANALYSIS

If we recognize placements in the college or the talent acquisition activities in the corporate as a serious process, we would give due weightage as well as respect to the entire activity and treat the same with more respect and concern.

The reason is simple.

The activity of mass hiring has changed the way the world sees us. So much so that the people world over fight for space in the process. The development of separate and dedicated verticals in all software giants and the Navaratna companies of the government of India bears testimony to this. The process of selection, training, absorption and subsequent retaining of freshers in organizations is a subject of some serious research. One striking reason for the success of the software corporates is that they never cribbed about the quality of the students, but absorbed the slightly better ones and then trained them seriously. They improved the quality while they paid the students. They did not wait for the government to do something. The rejuvenation of the Indian economy is due to this acquisition activity of corporates rather than any tinpot politician.

The accuracy of the process has the potential to create an impact for the generations to come.

If we go back just a few decades we can see the impact of placements in the software industry has left a mark on the overall picture of Indians and their present dominance in global commercial and technical activity. We have to actually consider the placements as a separate sector just like the other economic sectors in the economy. All the present boom in the economy owes a lot to the planning and execution of the placements by the software and a few other core industries.

If we study placements, we would find two major parts. One is the industry and the other is the institutions. The interphase between these two major activities is important. We can safely say that the talent acquisition people from the software industry have almost replaced the earlier versions of consultants who were offering jobs. The volume of employment they deal with in the software industry is incomprehensible for most in the field and outside. The turnover measured in money and numbers is simply fascinating. The students must be grateful to these visionaries who started the software industry. The impact has been seen in other sectors such as media, renewable energy, and even in simple manufacturing with respect to salaries and participation.

The training and placement officer read as a TPO, (as he is usually and more often derogatorily referred to by almost all who matter and those who do not) never ever really knows what a red-hot seat he is asked to occupy, at the beginning of his stint.

Most commonly a TPO is a fresh appointee in the college or someone is transferred as a punishment to this department. Whatever such a person does for the whole year nobody in the management gives a penny. There is very little guidance for him for two reasons. The first reason is that the principal, himself, does not know (in most institutes the principal is a rubberstamp) what is to be done by this department, and secondly, most teachers purposefully stay away from the process of placements, because they are fully aware of the *quality* of their teaching and the quality of the students.

In most colleges, the placement training is done by the humanities department people. You may ask "Why", and you may never get answers. The management has *not understood* even the basic *teaching* as a process so understanding of the *training* is far beyond *their limited comprehension*. The teacher and the principal both are ineffective as teachers, which is the main reason for the failure of students in the placements.

The common understanding about training is:

- a lot of pomp,
- smartly dressed, over-animated, English-speaking person,
- some self-promotion of the training person,
- filling in a lot of excel sheets, and yes, a lot of photographs, promotion in social media,
- reporting to the regulating authorities either in the state or the national capital, who are as ignorant as the Ph.Ds. in the institutions,
- The whole activity is conducted for the mandatory compliance of the regulatory bodies, rather than due to any genuine concern for the students.
- the training is considered an unnecessary expense rather than an investment

That is explained easily.

The ones who occupy the seats of chairman of such bodies are either uneducated or from the same unfit stable of academics. The good ones from the academics are working away from the campus and for the industry. The academics have no idea about the training process and even less idea about the actual placements. They keep a guided and intentional indifference to such a process and keep the students at the lowest step of the ladder. Even today the management in most colleges feels that a *Ph.D. is enough* for the training of students going for campus placement. Someone, teaching English or others who teach subjects like economics, history, and yes psychology can be good trainers. (If they do so in some exceptional cases, it is because of their individual aptitude, rather than their degree.) There are many who double up as trainers without knowing either teaching or training. The appointment of the trainers and the TPO generally gives a fair picture of the unfair activity run under the cation of T&P. If a routine survey is undertaken it would produce findings that would shake the basic foundations of this shabbily handled activity. Going by the general standards these resources are not properly equipped and they rarely know what they are doing. *Students, most importantly, also know the value of such sessions and they usually bunk these.*

Ever since private engineering colleges started operating in various states, the same routine of imparting training for preparing the students for various employability skills is conducted and the results are generally not anything to write home about. The scene does not change in an appreciable way because nobody seems to take any interest in the same. Again, if you really stretch and try, you may find some institutions that do appropriate and appreciable activities, but they are the exceptions.

There is something positive development also, at least the government now is planning for skill development, and a designated and hopefully dedicated ministry is started. *At least they have started talking* about it. Historically, India had a structured way of traditional skills and management. In the flow of time, we lost our advantages and blindly followed the systems which were and even today are detrimental to our culture, ethos, and way of living. The trainer has to go back in time and devote some time to learning the training methods in ancient India which were successfully prevalent for centuries before the unwanted and unwelcome intrusion of people who had evil designs for the destruction of one of the most successful systems of education and training. Generation after generation benefitted and transmitted the wisdom.

Why Indian students need special training for such basic things as corporate etiquette, communication, presentation, facing an interview, and many such aspects of an adult human life, is a question that needs to be answered at all levels of education. *Why there is a distinct mismatch between the marks scored by the students in the mark sheets and the basic comprehension levels of the students is one more haunting question to most of the trainers in the placement activity in the country.* The beginning has been made and we all seriously hope that something worthwhile churns out as a process that can be safely duplicated. The process of churning has no control over what comes out of the same. For example, the Amrit and Halahal (the poison) emerged from the same process as Samudra Manthan. So, some powerful and resourceful person should control the process. Again, there is a requirement of training not only for the average students say in the B and B+ category, but surprisingly the topper variety also needs guidance in the most common-sense aspects of life. The intent towards the self and self-development is simply absent. Most students whether graduate or post-graduate cannot talk about themselves even for a minute. Apart from academics, as they call it, these students of all varieties, distinctly lack the orientation and the urge to excel in their future corporate lives. It does not really matter whether they opt for the jobs or they walk the path of an entrepreneur, the fact remains that they would need the *best of the people's skills* if they wish to succeed in any appreciable way in their respective fields.

In any college where they teach engineering, management, medicine, pharmacy, science, humanities, law, or commerce the problems of attitude and aptitude are more or less the same. The difference would be mainly in the absorbing capacity of the students. The students with more quotient of basic intelligence would pick up things faster during the training sessions and with consummate ease, whereas the others would need a stressful effort from both the students and the trainers. Adult learning is best seen in the training sessions of the placement activity. The climb down from the attitude of 'I know it all to 'I need to improve and that too very fast is not easy to adapt. And when the students somehow accept the need to change, they find that the people who are supposed to handle the change are not very well equipped. Somehow with all faults in the system, most of the students absorb the training, in various degrees which reflects in their offer letters and salary packages. In fact, the B and B+ students adapt faster in comparison to the elite variety. The reason is the inside tussle with the inner uncompromising selves and the nonacceptance of the trainers, in the minds of the elite. The adjustment from the *pampered to the common* comes with a lot of deliberate effort. The acceptance of the fact that they need training comes with a lot of difficulties.

Comfort zones: One of the most commonly used terms in the context of the training is the 'comfort zone of a person. A person in this zone is either happy with what he is or he has accepted his lot. He does not expect anything better and tries to justify his sporadic success or usual failures. He says that due to a variety of reasons he would not succeed in anything new. He wilfully blocks any success stories around him and turns into an 'all-knowing- nothing doing' person. Such people in any group are dime a dozen and the only thing that they emit is a whole lot of negativities, in everything they are a part of. *Weeding out such people from any actionable group is the major concern of any trainer*. There are many cases in the present dynamic scenario of our economy which would stand for this hypothesis. Whether it is the core banking, private insurance companies, explosion in E-media, or the bustling education institutes, E-commerce all bear out the fact that they have problems in changing their people. The suddenness of the change required with reference to the pattern of working, the changes in the ownership, added responsibility, and serious reviews of the performances have proved quite an energy-draining factor. With management post-graduates working overtime, the organizations should have better planning but apparently, it is not so. Most managements are employing people not because they are good, but because their physical presence is needed. It is a pathetic fact. It is bound by some outdated rules and misconcepts. The speed needed for keeping up with the changing times is absent. The selection process does need a complete revamp or else all the organizations would face a serious crunch even of 'work- culture' human resources, much bigger than the present one, in the near future.

What can a trainer do with such people?

The question the trainer has to answer is whether is it worth spending time in improving such people or should he look for better alternatives.

What is more viable- *the training of the existing or the hiring of new people*?

Are any alternatives available?

If they are, what is the guarantee that in the course of time the presently 'better' would not transform into the 'all-knowing – anything doing' version?

Even if on a purely theoretical premise, it is possible to replace a person who is not developing into what an organization wants; in the reality, it is rarely done. The selection process, the subsequent time consumed in the training activity, the time spent in giving time to a person to prove that he is a misfit and the subsequently combined repeat of all the above activities in the case of a new appointee can dig a sizeable hole in the coffers of the organization. The problem lies in the fact that you may repeat the process and yet the results would always be erratic. A person in a comfort zone when confronted with a sudden change is frightened beyond limits. The problem can be divided into two parts. He knows that he is somehow coping with the tasks assigned to him, also that he is not good even if he is doing the same thing for years.

Secondly, he is distinctly aware that to learn to do anything new to manage the anticipated change he would have to stretch. *The problem starts and ends here.* Not for the trainers, though! The trainer faces one more problem. He may somehow find out a way, to make the students listen to what he has to say in the form of training imparted, but that in itself is rarely enough. The trained ones may know certain things and processes, in extra after the training session; they may even pass the exams with flying colors. They are, then, out of the bounds of the training department. They report to the respective in-charges in the various working departments. If they perform the contribution of the trainers is conveniently forgotten, but if the employees do not the in charge has a ready-made punching bag in form of the training department. The training person has no say in the selection of a candidate or an employee, he is not in the knowledge of the aptitudes and the attitudes of the trainees, in most cases he is not even aware of the fact the trainee is sent for training as a last chance to retain the employment. The trainer finds out very soon that a person who is to retire in the next three years is very reluctant to change. He has no administrative control and the whole training exercise in such a case turns into a farce. It takes the right combination of training skills and administrative efficacy to get something worthwhile from this imposed training. It is sad but that still remains the only way of motivation. All things the trainer knows and wishes to apply come to nothing. The policymakers in our country whether in the public or private sectors usually do not meet any resistance to anything they say. They have a readymade 'ji huzoor' force ready. Further, they do not welcome any voice, right or wrong, indicating dissent, barring very few bosses who are open to suggestions. This is a defeat of all management principles and can result in an irreparable loss of resources. The people are expected to change in a flash, expected to adapt from one function to the other, creating a huge tension. Take any policy decision in the last five decades and you would find that even after years the planned policy is not working. If it is at all working there are many casualties, which clearly indicates the failure of proper planning and its subsequent implementation. One of the basic principles of training is to make a trainee understand *'If you do what you have been always doing, you would always be what you always are*. The necessity of changing and the reasonable logic of the advantages of a change can be understood by all people if properly presented. This is one more assumption but most of the time it stands the test of time. So, the trainer and the management have to see that the training imparted is put, to 'the do mode', otherwise, the training sessions would produce the 'all-knowing –nothing doing' types which are more dangerous than simple 'doing nothing types. Standstill knowledge is as dangerous as a pool of stagnant water. Both can be a source of a whole lot of negative viruses. The only people who suffer from physical and organizational viruses are healthy and productive people.

The process of campus selection is well known to all involved and yet every year same mistakes are repeated without fail. Batch by batch, year after year, the students surprisingly fall into the same ditch very similar to their seniors. Each student has a fair idea about the resume, aptitude tests, GD, and PI and yet they perform very predictably poorly. The success rate is about ten to fifteen percent nationally, and if the **trainers apply the process in the correct way, they can raise the percentage to a safe forty percent or even more**. Most colleges who claim a hundred percent placements have smartly played with figures. It is more statistics than facts. If you look into the data a little more deeply you would know the hidden invisible parts. The placement process would be discussed in the forthcoming chapters. Here it would suffice to underline that the implementation of the process is more important than the *sticking-to-the-letter* approach. When you know that everyone, everywhere, and every time would be doing the same thing you need to distinguish. Remembering Shiv Khera's almost epic tagline saying "Winners don't do different things, they do it differently" helps a lot.

***

CHAPTER III

Training for Placements Idea and Concept

Training for Placements

Idea and Concept

Background –

It is now a matter of common knowledge that in spite of acquiring very high degrees and diplomas in various fields of education, very few people are really where they should be. The worse part in most such cases is that the concerned person is not even aware of the problem. The education the person receives, may at best, prepare him for getting a job.

Once equipped with a degree the person expects that his life shall automatically fall into the right groove and it is here, he gets his first real taste of disappointment and disenchantment. By the time he (or she) realizes that the education he, received with a lot of effort, expenses, aspirations, and time, is not by itself, enough to overcome the challenges thrown at him or by the ruthless world, he is very near to his active life. The inadequacy of formal education becomes evident either suddenly or in phases and then the following problems are found:

- Lack of soft skills: Soft skills these days have assumed great importance. It is projected as an ultimate tool for the improvement of the students without addressing the basic problems in education. The student who has some core knowledge of the subjects can be helped by the training in soft skills, not in a reverse way.
- Lack of language: The biggest issue is the lack of language. That too, English! Yes, it is a problem but that is not the whole issue. The students these days do not know any language in a worthwhile way including their mother tongue. How a student learns and passes the degrees without any working knowledge is beyond any logic.
- Lack of general awareness: The concept of current news awareness is missing. With all the explosion of information, the students know the unwanted things more than the relevant ones. It reflects when they appear for the selection. The current news awareness has two more steps. Such as the current news analysis and the current news application. The students who involve themselves in all three are more

acceptable in the selection process.

- Lack of structured thinking: Structured thinking is possible only when basic thinking is happening. Structured thinking includes the collection of data, collation of data, sequencing of the collected data, analysis of the data, and at last the all-important application of the data. Those who can do this entire process distinguish themselves in whatever they do in their lives.
- Lack of clarity of roles: The clarity of anything comes from the correctness of the knowledge one has. If the knowledge is just average, the students would be confused and never take any initiative.
- Lack of proper preparations: Most of the above need solid preparation. It includes stretching beyond the normal limits.

It is also observed that many of the students especially those who have graduated from smaller towns, generally find it extremely difficult to cope with the expectations and circumstances, mainly due to an assumed feeling of inadequacy. The beginning of their professional life almost always begins on a proverbial back foot, creating a lifelong backlog. Actually, if such students are trained in a proper way they develop into very capable managers.

The Plan:

The plan for the technical institutes would be different as compared to the management institutes. The technical students onward to the 5th semester would be trained. The intensity of the training would increase as the students approach the final semester.

Whereas the students from the MBA courses would be trained from the second semester and serious efforts would start once the students decide on the sector they want to work for.

In both cases, the training would be general, to begin with, and subsequently would become specific with respect to the sector, company, and even the function. The training is mainly to teach the students how to clear the interview and how to impress the person from the company.

With this premise, we have tried to develop the Quality Training Programme, which should help every student to realize his true potential. We are sure that subsequent to sincerely attending this carefully developed course the students shall be more confident and more importantly competent.

Objective:

- To know, face, and most importantly excel in the competition.
- Practical intelligence and common-sense management.
- Acquiring self-confidence through knowledge and experience.

Method:

Brainstorming sessions would be conducted using the interactive method of imparting knowledge.

- Role Playing
- Situational analysis
- Problem-solving
- Case studies
- Simulation as and when possible
- Mock interviews
- GD sessions
- And of course, the instruction from the teachers and trainers.

Course Contents.

Capsule 1

- You
- Your personality
- Your posture, the way you talk and walk
- Various types of personalities
- Your attitude.
- Your potential

Capsule 2

- You and your surroundings
- You as a part of the society
- You as an Indian citizen.

Capsule 3

- You and your formal education
- What are you supposed to know?
- The actual scenario.

Capsule 4

- You and your quest for knowledge
- Are you teachable?
- Accepted sources of knowledge

Capsule 5

- You and your communication skills
- Communication with self
- Self-talk
- Person to person
- Official
- Oration, debates, group discussions
- Meetings
- Addresses
- Key note speeches
- And others

Capsule 6

- You and your image
- Your impressions about you
- Beyond 15 minutes smartness
- Positive and negative attributes
- SWOT analysis
- Helping you to become what you want to be.

Capsule 7

- Competition
- Understanding competition
- Genesis, and tackling competition
- To excel without Jealousy
- Team spirit

Capsule 8

- Practical Intelligence
- Day to day smartness
- Handling the routines correctly
- Computer smartness

Capsule 9

Application of knowledge

- Importance of the actual action
- Learning a skill and using it to make money

Capsule 10

- Aspirations and Goals
- Goal setting.>>>> Impossible or slightly improbable
- Accomplishing the goals
- Continuous evaluation
- Reviews

Capsule 11

- Relationships
- The inner and outer self
- Living on different levels in life
- Managing colleagues and the boss
- Managing your success

Capsule 12

- How to get the job you want?

- Responding to the advertisements
- Interviews
- The complete process of selection and its pitfalls.

(12 x 2 hours/each capsule =24 hours)

It is expected that after attending and doing all practice sessions the students would be more confident and conversant with the process. Their fear of competition, incompetence, and interview would be greatly reduced if not eliminated.

Placements:

The real indicator of the success of any professional educational institute is the placements and the ease with which the students get the same. Is it in the third semester or later? Does corporate come to us or do we have to approach them? Are the expectations of the students satisfied or a compromise is accepted? These are some of the questions we have to sincerely answer.

The placement market is predominantly divided into two major categories. The first is the Government and the second but equally important is the private industries. Maybe, we are trying to compensate for the loss in the government sector by being aggressive in the private sector.

Training is the foremost activity. It should be designed in such a way that the student has a general idea of how an industry works, what are the routine industrial processes, finance, and its implications, and HR and its role. We train for general placement. However, if the student wants a better placement, then he should be ready to **stretch** well beyond the normal routine and take the intensive training made available to him.

Training has to be comprehensive; it should be the same across the country. At the same time, we have to avoid Regimentalisation. We have to look into the originality of each student. If we say that a student is in the "A" category then it should automatically mean that he has achieved excellence in the pre-decided criteria. The parameters have to be centrally designed and more importantly controlled without depending on the Local Effect, which is not always rational.

The demand side has to be on a steady scale. Regular demand rather than a spike here or a boom there really helps. A regular check-up on the repeat demands and the referrals would be always very helpful.

The past students and their happiness levels are to be monitored. This activity should at least rope in 15 percent of job offers.

Before identifying the training needs, we have to seriously divide the available sample of students into categories. Say something like A, B, and C. The training needs of these students are different. The trainer has to keep all his trainees interested so he must have a fair idea about the capacity and the interest levels of the students.

This process would be completed before the students re-join, the campus after the summer vacations. The college would give the relevant data in the format.

The pre-placement interviews would start right from the first month of the 5th semester and each student would be given feedback along with correction tips.

- The training needs and their identification
- The training, as a process.
- The evaluation, as a process.
- Mid-Course corrections.

The training needs:

The most important training need is the core subject knowledge and its application. What you know you may not be able to express. In all specializations of the BE, the students are expected to talk sensibly about their subjects. With very little conscious effort put in, the students find the effort very challenging, and mostly first few interviews are wasted just for learning what is expected. We can save this time by proper expectations management of the students.

Secondly, all students are essentially at similar intellectual, maturity, and exposure levels which cuts a very sorry picture, especially at the campus level interviews.

The training process: The process of the training would be composite, integrated, and interdisciplinary and would include all the recent techniques as well as the proven techniques including reading and writing.

The evaluation process: The evaluation would be a continuous type and would facilitate the students for a mid-course correction.

The mid-course corrections: Whenever any new technique or input is found useful the same would be incorporated to extract maximum benefit for the students.

Commitment is essential for the students to at least practice. The trainers cannot practice for the students.

Role of 'Image and its Management' in placements.

Image Building: The Image is what people think you are. It is different than Identity. Images tend to be gradually developed and perceived whereas identity is quickly observed. Images are evolutionary and are made better as the organization achieves the intended progress. Identities on the other hand can be created on the drawing board, carefully pieced together, and most importantly controlled. Traditionally Corporate Identity and the image as an extension of the identity focused on the Name and the graphic expression of the brand. However, the challenge today is to build a broad-based worldwide image. Corporate image is the perceived sum of the entire organization, its present and future plans, and even its objectives. The total includes the products, services, style of management, the communication of the philosophies, and its subsequent actions across the country or the globe. The organization projects itself through its products, its brands, its images, the logos, the messages it gives to the customers, and most importantly corporate actions both inside and outside the establishment. Building a positive corporate image requires skillful long-term planning. If achieving a homogeneous acceptable image is difficult then sustaining the same is much more difficult and requires a sustained and conscious effort.

When the thinking of the outside people is to be modified as per the requirements of the organization, it becomes the Image Building. The significant activity is divided into two major sub-areas, which are Internal and external images of all the persons concerned.

The internal image is mainly reflected in the opinions of the students, faculty, and staff whereas the external image is in the minds of the industry, other competitive institutions, common people, students other than PCE, and even the Government.

Action Plan Proposed.

Improve the ambiance.

- Homogeneity of the thoughts and information to be disseminated.
- Put proper and correct information in the minds of those who are involved in the operations of the Institution.
- Student participation in the form of student placement forum.

Proper information such as

- Positives of **ABC INSTITUTE OF TECHNOLOGY**
- The extent of the activities of the **ABC INSTITUTE OF TECHNOLOGY**
- The uniqueness of **ABC INSTITUTE OF TECHNOLOGY**
- Mostly the input of the students is at –B or B level. Subsequently, they are made ready to compete with the top classes.
- The shift has to be from the **problem mode to the pride mode. The pride in being a part of ABC INSTITUTE OF TECHNOLOGY**

- Instead of a cohesive effort, most of the brand-building activity is done under compulsion instead of conviction.
- The overall attitude of the staff, and teachers, has to undergo a change. They may give a very wrong impression to the students and outsiders. The students watch very carefully the actions of all of us.
- Any institute becomes great only when the students are accepted by society. The building and the infrastructure are secondary. The students are the direct output, interacting with society.
- The alumni and their contribution to the process have to be nurtured.

The working of lectures and manpower planning can be worked out at a later stage once the plan is approved or suitably modified as per the requirements.

The approach: Depending upon the time, money, and inclination we can have two suitable alternatives. At first, we can develop a single module dedicated to one institute, and later the same can be replicated for the entire Institution activity.

Or

We can start simultaneously in all colleges and correct the procedure while in operation.

***

CHAPTER IV

The TPO and his work cut-out

The TPO and his work cut-out

(Development of ignorant students, disinterested teachers, casual administration, and demanding recruiters, yet producing results season after season.)

The job profile of a TPO

The job profile of the training and placement officer is very interesting. Two random examples are taken from Google. One is from India and one is from a foreign institute. They make interesting reading. It is seriously doubted how many of the education management can really comprehend the same.

For example:

- To look after the training and placement activities of students ·
- To have close liaison with industry for the placement of students. ·
- To work in consultation with the coordinator Industry –Institute interaction for organizing lectures from the professionals and industry. ·
- To collect feedback from the companies coming for placement ·
- Arrange training programs for soft skills and for interview-facing skills for the students using institutional and external expertise.
- Organize entrepreneurship training/workshops. To evaluate all activities on a continuous basis and implement mid-course corrections to reach a pre-decided target.

Or

one more sample

1. Implement job placement services for students and graduates; design programs as part of the curriculum for job-seeking skills; make classroom presentations as requested.

2. Plan, direct, and oversee studies to evaluate vocational/technical students and programs. Perform research and longitudinal studies on students, graduates, and employers for State reports.

3. Contact potential employers by telephone, written correspondence, and site visits to promote the programs of the college or continuing

education centers to identify and develop career positions related to academic/vocational preparation; full and part-time, paid, and non-paid internships, and other off-campus employment.

4. Supervise assigned employees; appraise performance, provide technical direction and guidance, and make employment recommendations.

5. Provide career advisement to students, including but not limited to career goals, requirements of specific occupations, job market trends, proper work habits, and techniques for competing for jobs, including appropriate grooming and dress, effective methods for completing job applications and preparing resumes, and interviewing methods.

6. Facilitate the interviewing of students to assist in the completion of placement assistance request forms; maintain files of student applicants; conduct pre-screening of students to verify qualifications.

7. Supervise the receiving of job orders from employers; match students to jobs and maintain records of students placed in jobs.

8. Analyze available job market economic data and information. Research job market trends and requirements for a variety of occupations.

9. Coordinate contractual relationships with a variety of government-funded programs.

10. Serve as a member of committees concerned with the coordination of job placement services.

11. Perform special studies as requested.

12. Perform related duties as assigned.

The desirable traits

1. Knowledge: Applicable sections of California Education Code.
2. Basic research and statistical methods.
3. English usage, grammar, spelling, punctuation, and vocabulary.
4. Federal and State employment and compensation laws.
5. Job development and placement methods and techniques.
6. Labor market conditions and trends.
7. Modern office practices, procedures, and equipment, including computer hardware and software.
8. Oral and written communication skills.
9. Principles and practices of training and supervision.
10. Principles of marketing.
11. Principles of public administration and management planning.
12. Technical aspects of the field of specialty.

Skills and Abilities:

1. Analyze situations accurately and adopt an effective course of action.
2. Communicate effectively both orally and in writing.
3. Conduct research, create data, analyze data, and prepare reports. Conduct reviews and take remedial actions.
4. Establish and maintain effective working relationships with others.
5. Identify key requirements of occupations and skills relative to college and continuing education programs.
6. Monitor, develop, and allocate assigned budgets.
7. Networking within the community to publicize and promote offerings of colleges/continuing education.
8. Read, interpret, and explain labor laws, affirmative action, wage, and salary regulations.
9. Relate effectively with people from varied cultural and socio-economic backgrounds.
10. Work independently with little direction.

What is your take on this?

One of my friends said that it looks like a constitution of a small-time nation. Come to think of it and you are more than surprised that most colleges have the junior most or an inconsequential person as the TPO. What is the need? Anybody can do the job! The management just does not have time to think about this expense. They are more concerned about counting money and increasing revenue. If we go to the academic management of the college most Principals or the HODs have no inkling about this aspect of education. They conveniently forget that it is because of their inept handling of education that the need for the training and placement department has arisen. They keep a safe distance from this department. Yes, they reserve all ridicule and sarcasm but very rarely contribute. Again, there are welcome exceptions but they are rare.

The actual work

When the TPO takes charge, he rarely knows the dimensions of the job. Leave aside the depth at which he would be needed to work. All the promises of the talents, backgrounds both academic as well as the family, and such things as a discipline are as credible as the election promises of the typical Indian Neta. After about a week or so, the TPO starts to move. He generally is not mature enough or very mature to avoid the job.

So, for the sake of all such TPO fraternity let us have a snapshot of what is needed to do.

- The time frame: - The first thing he has to find out is the time frame of the process. If he starts sometime around June or July and if the academic sessions have started on time, he has about four to six months. The time span depends mainly upon the placement season which is controlled by some companies who block the colleges by the norm called Day one. One more organization used to be effectively called NASSCOM, in addition to UGC, NAC, and AICTE. Right in the induction stage, the TPO has to know, understand, and coordinate the external and internal environment. For the external, he is not known and in the internal environment, he does not matter. The people in the ivory towers in the college rarely bother to even get introduced and leave aside helping. So, in this step, the TPO should be aware of his rare friends and hope that they remain his friends till the conclusion of the placement season sometime around February next year.
- The preparation on the college side: - The first and most important step involves the TPO. He is the first person who needs complete faith in the process, students, management, and the support staff. Any doubt in his mind would hamper the complete process whether everybody puts in the best effort. The TPO needs to know the complete picture and the rest on a need-to-know basis. One more thing which is very vital is the complete faith and support of the top management in the function of the TPO and the financial support. *Any deviation here is a sure failure.* The Placement season is long and the TPO needs course correction and booster doses to sustain the known and unknown pressures. The job is not easy. It involves everyone. The management should ensure that at least the internal factors do not work against the objective of placing the students in the best possible organizations. It is seen that the teaching staff always keeps a guided distance from the TPO. At least until some placements actually occur. They pounce on the credit cake subsequently.
- Before the season begins: -

  a. Data accumulation- The data of the students are generally available from the college registrar or the administrative officer. At least that is told to the TPO. He finds that either easily or with a lot of effort depending upon the culture of the college. He needs branch-wise students or an MBA specialization-wise. This is his first official task.

b. Data analysis- He needs to segregate the students on the basis of what the future employer wants. The various parameters are

- Age
- Sex
- Any disability
- Mother tongue
- Languages competency
- Medium of instruction
- Family background
- Place of stay
- Branch
- Marks at the tenth, twelfth, graduation, and semester wise
- Extra-curricular activities
- Publications if any
- Participation at any national or international competitions
- Certifications like JAVA, C++, PYTHON, .NET, AUTOCAD, DESIGNS
- And any other relevant and topical detail required by the employer.

c.- ABC analysis of the student data- Of all the preparations this step is the most important as it gives a clear picture to the TPO. He knows what he is dealing with.

ABC is categorising the students on the basis of grades.

"A" Grade students would have

-60% percent marks in 10th /12th / and the qualifying exam of 6th or 7th semester

-All clear subjects

- Language proficiency

Some companies these days demand 65% or even 70% as the cut off.

Some companies exempt students above 80% from the preliminary rounds of aptitude tests or Group discussions. They select on the basis of the personal interview.

B -Grade students would have deficiencies in one or two aspects as per the above parameters.

C-grade students would be having nothing of the parameters stated above.

The TPO has to be very patient with all these categories. They present different types of problems or more fashionably challenges. The A students would be choosier and fussier, so they expect special service. Their expectation management would turn out as the toughest job. The B is more confused and needs special attention to make them believe that they have a more than a fair chance to succeed in the race and get suitable placement. The C-category students are the worse hit. They are the ones who have lost the race even before it is begun. Their conversion from C to B is very difficult. Their wish is just a job.

- Contacting the probable corporates or companies: -The standard procedure is to send a standard introductory mail to all the employers. The mail needs to be designed, edited, and made as best as possible. One word of caution is to stick to facts as far as possible. The talent acquisition people are smart and can see through the bluff very easily. Do not oversell the product. To evoke a worthwhile response the number of emails should never be limited. It is estimated that about ten thousand companies exist in the sector so the TPO should arrange to get their email ids and send the email to all of them. The Email IDs should be authentic otherwise the whole exercise would be futile.

Another way is through the student alumni.

Or the TPO can use the previous year's employers or the companies which visited the college.

Or the TPO can request the Professors, teachers, or even the students to provide the Email IDs of the people they know.

Just like the students, the TPO must rate the companies into ABC. He should never assume or have fixed ideas about where he would be getting placements. He has to understand that a man from a relatively lesser-known company can give him a reference for a larger, well-known giant of a company. The TPO must work like a missionary or follow the path of karma yoga. He should just send as many emails as possible and hope for the best.

- Weekly Roadmap: As discussed earlier in this chapter it helps to decide the number of weeks, he would have in the placement season. If he is lucky, he would have about twenty weeks. So, if he wants to work smart, he has to plan week-by-week activities and work on them. A sample is given which would need local editing and customized details.

- <u>Week 1</u>: Data collection and its correction. The resume activity must be finished. The final version of the resumes to be submitted is a must. The training for the placement-seeking students to start. The introduction and knowing the people involved. Such as the students, the teachers, the staff at the T&P cell, and most importantly the Principal and the Directors of the college. A clear-cut understanding of their expectations is a MUST.
- <u>Week 2</u>: The first round of mock interviews must start this week. It may not be very productive but it would set the ball rolling. The aptitude tests must also be conducted internally. The results of the ATs as they are called are a real eye-opener for the students and their teachers. The training in soft skills must start this week.
- <u>Week 3</u>: The sector analysis of the possible employment opportunities. Unless the TPO knows and has a grip on which sectors he needs to cater it would be very difficult to strategize the future course. As of today in 2022, the following sectors show tremendous promise in the next fifteen years to come. They are

    - Medicare
    - Forestry
    - Mining
    - Education and training
    - E-learning like the Byju etc
    - Traveling/tourism

The others with average growth would be the real estate, IT, and infrastructure industries.

The point to understand is none of the data is fully dependable. Also, it is available to all in the field. It is totally up to the TPO to analyze, and align his efforts so that he has a happy ending.

- <u>Week 4</u>: Simultaneously, he must have by now sent at least one thousand emails to the companies in the IT sector, core industries, and service industries. The Email itself needs a lot of smart drafting. He may take help from many but the final draft has to be his own. What is the USP of his students, the last three years' performance, and the preparation of his students, are some of the pointers? He should never bluff in this correspondence. Actually, the rule is never to bluff about a matter which can be easily verified. For example, never brag about the quality of the students, and never lie about the quality of the teachers. Talent acquisition people are smart they catch up with the facts very soon. The TPO has to always remember that he is a matchmaker. He provides what is available. He has not produced or taught and he has limited control over the finished products. At best he can refurbish the outer core and make the product more presentable. He should be involved in the activities but he should know his limit.

- Week 5: By week five the first stage of the entire process should be finished.

The emails must have been sent, the follow-ups started, the talks about DAY 1,2,3 and so on should be started.

All students must have faced at least *one mock interview* and shown their shortfalls.

The Aptitude Tests must be smoothly conducted.

The trainers must have conducted sessions on GDPI. And they submit their observations on the individual students. Again, it has a limited value. The TPO has to devise his own methods to evaluate the students. The trainers in all colleges are generally raw and compromised. There are exceptions but they just prove the rule.

- Week 6: In the sixth week if the TPO is really lucky he would have some placements done. That helps a lot. He can use his resources and arrange for military service interviews. The Pre SSB type. They help in many ways. The students can be absorbed in the armed forces. But they also present the best opportunity for mock interviews. The people from the army are the best in the business and the students are benefitted immensely.

The activities presented in the six weeks are to continue simultaneously. Like a seasoned project manager, the TPO has to keep track of all activities and control with an iron fist. He should send follow-up mails to his stakeholders and seek action. The emails are better than talks.

The same pattern would continue in all twenty weeks, but as the end of the season approaches the tension, the stress, the frustrations, or the joys may increase.

- Consoling the rejected students: One of the most neglected activities in the placement process is the handling of the rejected student. The TPO is the only one who can break open his vault of disappointment, frustration, and even jealousy. What the TPO does in those ten-twenty minutes interactions with the rejected student, is the crux of his job. He has to be concerned, but he should not over-sympathize. He has to regenerate the hope in the mind of the student and if possible, make him participate in the immediate next placement drive. He should be pepped up and made to understand that getting rejected by one or two companies is a part and parcel of the process. He should cite examples from the last batches.
- Follow up with the corporates.: TPO has to understand that he and the corporates are the constants in the process and the students are the variables. So, he must have a great relationship with all the HRs, Talent Acquisition Managers, and higher-ups in the companies. In fact, he should be able to reach the other side and make sure that he is treated with some respect. The relationship must be really solid.
- Alumni: The TPO should be a respected person in the Ex-student's community who was preferably placed earlier. The bond between the properly placed student and the TPO can be one of the strongest bonds. Most students have acknowledged the role played by the TPO in providing them with the initial impetus in their careers. The *alumni* as it is called is an *untapped resource in most colleges.* If handled properly, the college may never need to prospect the industry as over a period of time the alumni of the colleges are occupying top management positions and are in a position to help their alma mater. The record of the alumni needs to be updated all around the academic year. The alumni know the in and out of the college and when he refers the current batch of students, it creates a solid positive impact and works very favorably. At present most interaction with the alumni is limited to a shabbily arranged alumni meet time very inconvenient for the alumni. If there are exceptions, they again prove the rule. The indifference created by the circumstances needs to be converted into something near to pride and gratefulness.

The job is neither easy nor the time. There has to be a monthly activity, which should be necessarily treated as an investment rather than as an expense. It may be virtual, or in person but the past students must be included in the placements loop, as it is one of the surest and safest ways to get students placed in a verified company with a great reference.

The faculty and the academic staff: Whatever the responses of the teachers and other people in academics it is very essential for the TPO to harness the relationship with the teaching staff. TPO must understand:

- the insecurity in the minds of the teachers and the reasons for the same,
- their ego systems,
- their boring routine,
- the general waning respect of the students towards the teachers,
- their indifference towards the T&P activity

TPO can remember the famous saying of the Indian Prime Minister about the neighboring countries we have. Similarly, TPO *cannot choose* his faculty, but he can certainly find out those teachers who share his views and create a bond.

Finally, the TPO should never claim credit for the placements.

His credit line must be *we*instead of *me*.

***

CHAPTER V

Expectations Management

Expectations Management

They say in the HR circles that it is very rare that *good companies would get good candidates or that good candidate gets good companies.* It is a pretty profound statement and can be a debatable one. The problem is in human nature, where it tries to respond to many things which keep on changing situation by situation. The circumstances during the selection process are altogether different than what is presented to the candidate after his induction, similarly, the appearance of the student which led to his selection can be very deceptive. So, hoping that the student or the organization would hopefully cope with each other is very impractical. The selection of the candidates is a result of processes more dependent upon the law of averages. They include a sizeable number of those who would not be able to live up to the expectations of the management. The word, *expectations*, assumes great importance in the overall process of T&P. It includes the expectations of the students and the corporates.

The TPO has to manage his side of the deal. The expectations of the students need to be asked for, *downsized* most of the time, and even challenged by the TPO well before the actual interaction of the students with the companies. A student with mixed-up priorities and unreasonable expectations from the future life or company can be very frustrated with the process of selection.

In the case of the engineering student, it is a matter of his information and the source of the same. His expectations are based on the mixed and diverse inputs of his parents, senior students, his peers, and some teachers as well as his relatives. These days one can add the internet as a potent contributor. The feedback on the net can play a big role. There is a shade of ridicule rather than facts, in most of them. They give him unnecessary details about how Indian engineers are not up to. How only ten percent are actually employable.

One point is that generally, nobody is overly critical about what he has been doing so far. Actually, they convey their feelings to him that nothing much is expected of him while in college and he is in for doom in the future. So, he either is in a state of false and empty super overconfidence or he is at the bottom of self-esteem. In the first, he believes that he is the best and he deserves the best company with the best package, while in the other he is convinced that he is the duffer of the century.

Both cases are bad for the TPO.

Even before the TPO starts dealing with the expectations of the students he has to deal with the management of expectations of the principal, teachers, and even the non-teaching staff. The TPO is involved in the meetings for the expectations which he finds unreasonable, to say the least.

He is simply astonished that right from the day he assumes charge of the department everything is to be done by him. The students would be changed as if by the famous Pygmalion effect. Their MTI, LOC, LODK, postures, textures, lack of communication, lack of English, and many other complexes would be wished away. The management just washes away its hands and expects that 100% placements occur, that too in group A companies, with the best packages so that the next year's admissions are assured. After all, they are in the *business for the revenue* not for anything else like imparting education. In fact, the TPO realizes that whatever is written in the *mission statements* is diametrically opposite of what they actually want. Further, he realizes that they have not even read the same. The parents forget the realistic ability of their child, they forget that they had to pay a hefty capitation fee even for his admission, which in simple words means that he was not up to the required standards. The principal forgets the manipulations in the attendance, internals, practicals, the quality of his teachers, the ever-present holidays, and the lack of attitude in the students and the teachers. The Teachers who are mostly rueing over the fact they were either not selected in the industry, or if they were selected, they could not perform as per the high standards, hence shown the door, *play* their part in downsizing the confidence levels of the students. Their famous dialogue of telling *what is not possible* in their college or how the *students do not deserve any placements* kills the lowest level of optimism left in the minds of the students. In some cases, the teachers, generally do not say anything but what they *do not say* can be a great dampener. One look from such a teacher and the student community knows, that they heading toward doom. The silence is killing. The disinterest is heavy. Their running away from the very process of placements is frightening. Their frustration is so obvious that even the dumbest of students learn to avoid and neglect such people. Even when students get excellent placements and above-par packages these people remain morose. They cannot adjust to the fact that the students, who were dumb have outclassed their teachers in the most important part of life.

The role of non-teaching staff is not to be undermined. The fact that the T&P activities are generally held outside the academic schedule means some extra work. And like any Indian staff working in the offices, they do not at all like the extra bit of load. It disturbs their easy-paced lives. They resist every move, that too in a very administrative excuse way. The library does not help. The computer lab people behave in a peculiar way. The LCDs, the sound systems, and the mikes rarely work as they should. They work as if they are sure of the sorry results awaited in the future.

The grapevine and the gossip are in top gear. Every little bit of failure on the part of the TPO is reported to the willing ears. The reporter never forgets to add the mirch masala.

In fact, the TPO realizes that all of the above stakeholders are hoping that he fails as his earlier editions failed. Or otherwise, they neglect him as if he does not exist.

The beginning of the solution lies in the effort of reviving the interest in the minds of the three major stakeholders apart from the students. How does it happen? It is not easy.

The TPO has to be smart.

He has to generate some basic confidence. He should talk about the good old days when the college was in demand, admissions were bumper and the placements were ok. He has to use the tactic of praising the small little things. He has to create a feeling, where the stakeholders feel that things would be bright even if they would not participate. And that their reputation would be maintained. They know that if the placements do occur the entire credit would be falling into their laps.

Secondly, he has to identify the friendly people in his college. *It is highly impossible that all of them are all bad.* Some of them would exactly like the ideal ones needed for the job. They would be friendly, optimistic, ready to put in extra effort, ready to talk to students, and to somewhat share their confidence that if the students put in some effort they would be suitably placed. On that day when the students do not really know about the TPO, these helping hands would do wonders.

Thirdly the TPO needs to start the basic training activity, in which he should include activities that are simple and the students would be able to finish. It is always a good feeling that "I can do something" and later on the difficulty levels should be increased.

One bad word from the people who matter can act as a lump of salt added to a pot full of milk. The purpose of the entire activity is to ensure that the stakeholders would not harm the process if they do not help. That in itself is a big help.

Students:

Expectations management of the students is relatively easy. The reason is simple. Their emotions are pure, moreover, they want something out of the placement process. So, maybe, they are more prone to listen to what the TPO has to say.

The first step in the management of expectations is to accept them as it is. NEVER ARGUE about the logic of why he wants what he wants. What the student knows or does not the TPO need not go into details.

The approach is simple.

Ask him to write down what he wants.

What are his preferences?

Is there any dream company where he would like to work?

Or does he want to start his own venture?

Nobody should question why?

Nobody should tell him that he cannot get what he wants.

Once, he has written, ask him the easiest way to get the same.

How does he propose to accomplish what he wants?

Talking and writing are two different things. While talking he can just shoot off but when he is made to write many things automatically get filtered even at his levels. The things which survive the screening are slightly more refined and workable.

Explain to him, his time frame and ask him to fit his wishes against the same. Whatever he wants from the placement process has to be done in a maximum of 120 to 150 days. Ask him to convert the span into weeks. Ask him to submit his weekly *to-do* schedule. Work with him on the same and suggest some modifications, get his okay, and then ask him to follow. Tell him that you are available for this particular activity 24x7 and he is welcome to call.

The TPO has to put in extra effort in differentiating between wishful thinking and the practical choices presented by the companies. Getting a job is not like buying a lottery ticket, and even if a lucky student is selected by a company where the work allotted is beyond the capacity, he is very uncomfortable and most likely get the *dreaded pink slip* very soon.

The same exercise is to be repeated with all students irrespective of ABC categories.

In short, the expectations management is to make them understand what is available, what are the industry norms, and what they can achieve at what level of effort, and then let them put in their own directed hard work. The students understand the approach. They know what they are, where they stand, what help is available, what is the best option, and how to prepare for the same.

The preparation for the software and the core companies is different. The process is also slightly different. *The big difference is in the payment patterns.* But the students in the core sectors seem to work in the sector they were prepared for.

One thing which helps in the process is the *periodical mock interviews* of the students. The students keep on changing their choices and preferences so fast, but at least the TPO is aware of the changes. From the day of registration in the placement process and the day when the offer letter is handed over mock interviews is the only exercise that helps both parties. The student immediately knows where he stands and the TPO knows the correction and fine-tuning path.

The expectation management is to get the student to want what we want them to want but they should think that they would get what they want.

Once this ground preparation is ready the TPO would shift his attention to the general procedure of the training, which would further filter the students.

***

CHAPTER VI

Stakeholders and their Perspectives

Stakeholders and their Perspectives

In any process when we study, one aspect is the stakeholders who are a part of the process. What significance can be attached to each of them is a matter of individual assessment. Placements in educational institutions have many aspects which need special attention, but none can be more important than the stakeholders. Let us find out!

1. The college management
2. The HODs.
3. The teachers.
4. The administration.
5. The students
6. The parents

Let us analyse them one by one.

1. **The college management**: The primary stakeholder is the management of the college. The management in the colleges comprises the chairman, board of directors., secretary, and principal. In NITs and IITs the top man is the director. The acumen and the prejudices of these people really matter. The other thing which controls so many things, persons and processes in the T&P is the fact that these people pay. They control the finances required for the six-month-long placement season. That they are with or without the requisite knowledge is a matter of real concern. If they are educated and enlightened the T&P process is facilitated and the TPO is very fortunate to have such support. Very few management people are interested in the actual process of training or for that matter placements. Most of these people look at training as an unnecessary expense. For such an impression we cannot blame them fully. When they were in the initial phase and when they were enthusiastic, they were literally robbed of their money and belief by many professional training companies located across the country. They spent huge amounts and the subsequent results were disappointing. So, they are wary and

disinterested.

Secondly, they are a victim of a process called instant gratification. That a student needs some time and more importantly some specific training is beyond their normal reasoning.

Thirdly, in most cases, they are surrounded by clever people (chamchas) who would make the management spend millions on the infrastructure and some other areas which can be avoided.

Fourthly, they have almost forgotten that they are dealing with students who are impressionable and can at best concentrate on worthwhile things for a very short time span. There is no fixed ratio of input and output in the students as they have an issue of lack of preparation and very high expectations.

Fifthly, they expect that the T&P must be enthusiastic, and produce hundred per cent placements in any which way possible so that they can have a super admission season.

1. **The HODs**: The HODs in any professional college belong to a very particular creed of human beings. They are extremely egoistic. They almost feel that the world is in place because of them. They know that most problems in the college are due to a lacklustre attitude between them and the rest of the teaching staff, but they would never accept the same. For them, T&P is an activity of which they are never a part. They can see a TPO and they can never actually see him. Again, there are some welcome exceptions, but they merely prove the rule. More than the students the TPO spends more time convincing these people that he is doing something worthwhile. They may have their valid reasons but most of the time they refuse to understand that they could have been more effective while they taught and could have created a better human sample of students who were at least teachable. They forget that they spend maximum time with the students and yet they rarely get involved in the academic and social behaviour of the students. They crib about the input quality, lack of language, lack of facilities and many other things but they conveniently forget that all students on the first day of college are exactly like what they want. The students were youthful, excited, energetic, and dreamy but reduced to a deflated, dejected, and disappointed lot in the following years. A separate book can be written about *what* is the state of the teachers and what it *should be* so as to

improve the chances of the students getting properly placed. The domain knowledge or the lack of the same is the sole responsibility of the HODs. All their qualifications, intelligence, published articles, and sessions taken in foreign universities is useless if their student lacks basic subject knowledge.

2. **Teachers**: The teachers can be a great help to the T&P if they contribute positively. The students in spite of everything would listen to the teachers rather than anyone else. The teachers must understand that the students are in no way responsible for the not-so-good lots of the teachers. That the teachers do not get salaries as per the norms, that they have to do a lot of things they would avoid for the management, that they did not get a better job, that their English is pathetic, that they have very low self-esteem, that they are bitter about their life, that they have nothing to look forward to, is not because of the students. But due to peculiar circumstances, the students suffer the most and wonder why. One rule, if the teachers were to follow lots of the students would improve. The rule is to forget everything that is depressing, once inside a class and deliver the best in the class. It is the primary duty of the teachers to keep the interest of the students focused on the right things. All reasons and logics fade in front of the students and their future. In case of extremes, the concerned teachers must say goodbye to teaching, so that the students are protected from unwanted and dangerous negative feelings from the teachers.
3. **The Administration**: The administration department which includes the accounts, the registrar, the laboratory staff, the library staff, the security staff, the student's welfare department, and some other departments can contribute a great deal to the process of placements. The security staff at the gate can be a great first impression for anyone visiting the college for the first time. Each person in all these departments can provide worthwhile support to TPO in getting the students placed. The proper flow of money from the accounts, the uninterrupted power supply when the campus drive is on, and the general welcoming attitude towards the visiting company officials can help the college T&P department immensely.
4. **The students**: The students form the CORE of the entire T&P activity. They rarely realise this simple fact. The entire rigmarole is for the placement of the students. The disinterest of the students can be due to many reasons, which need to be identified and eliminated by the TPO.

Or else the result is already a foregone conclusion.

The students form a peculiar community. They tend to form opinions very fast, react even faster and generally repent later. They are not inclined to believe in their teachers, principal and the TPO. The reasons can be many and not always the students are to be blamed. The usual disinterest, the casual attitude, the apparent overconfidence and many such symptoms are observed in a majority of the colleges. The exceptions are a few and they benefit on a great scale.

It is suggested to the students that they must participate in all training activities even if they initially appear useless, and boring. The understanding comes to students that they are not ready when they go through the entire process. Students must understand that they are not as smart as they think they are. Each step in the training process, if they participate properly would make them more conversant with it and they would be ready. It is *better to fail in the earlier stages*, while you are in college when it really *does not* matter. They would know at each failure that they can improve and when the actual campus drive happens, they would be at ease, well-rehearsed and confident. They would know what to expect and go through the process successfully.

The students must understand the need for a script. They feel that the interview is easy but it is not so. The script with required variations depending upon the nature of the company which visits can help to gel properly, with the interview team.

The students must understand that any negativity about the college kills their chances to get selected.

They should be very careful about what they learn from their senior students who *could not get* the placements. They would obviously blame everyone except themselves. Their negativity is bad.

The domain subjects, their knowledge or lack of it, have a great impact on getting selected or otherwise. The knowledge of the domain is the only common ground that the interviewer shares with the student. Rest everything in the interview is very much student specific.

The projects, paper presentations, and participation on national and international levels can help in getting selected. Additional certifications in the specialization can certainly help. Aptitude tests form the major selection step and no student takes them seriously. The average selection or the hit ratio of the selections is less than ten per cent. This means that after each aptitude test only ten out of a hundred students can participate in the GD and PI sessions. It hurts. The simple rule of preparing for the ATs is **sixty aptitude tests in six days with a minimum score of 85 out of 100.**

Regular rehearsals of group discussions, and interviews, can be a crucial factor in getting selected.

6. **The Parents.** Present days parents can be very demanding of their wards and of the colleges. They want that their children must get good jobs and sky-high packages. Nothing wrong with such expectations. What hurts is that they do not have any logical support for the same. A load of undue expectations has reduced many young men into zombies. Yes, the parents have paid fees, in many cases the capitation fees, but that is not enough. They have to find time to be just with the kids.

In fact, it is seriously felt that the parents must be counselled even before the students. One thing the parents forget to assure their children is that they would continue to love their children even if they fail. The tension would be greatly reduced if the parents stand firmly with the children and support them.

Apart from the above society, the neighbours, the relatives, and many others who actually should not matter affect the process and the performance of the students. The TPO has to be very clever, he has to understand that people say a lot of things without really meaning them. The cliché used by the people around him needs to be decoded. So long as they are consistent, he has fewer worries. When things start becoming tougher the responses of all of the above would be changing. They would not want to be a part of the process and be responsible. They would be shifting the blame squarely on the TPO. The TPO must follow the example of *neer kshir vivek,* which tells us the capacity of the king swan to choose only milk and leave the water from the pot of milk. TPO needs to absorb better ideas, and suggestions and discard the usual unnecessary opinions, criticism, and adverse comments.

TPO has to be patient and understand that he has to do what he has to and keep doing the same such as improving the CV/ practice sessions for the AT/ more and more GD sessions and mock interviews. The students need to remain focused and that is supremely important. As soon as the students begin to be placed once again the language of the above would change. It is a simple matter of weathering the stress which is better done by the TPO.

***

CHAPTER VII

Role of a Trainer in the process of placements.

Role of a Trainer in the process of placements.

Ideally, the role of a placement trainer is very central in the overall process of getting your students placed. Please note the word placement. People argue about saying that there are many other trainers or guest lecturers who contribute to the process. Maybe, they do but they are never held accountable. The whole onus of responsibility falls on the placement trainer. He assumes the role of a Sutradhar. He is the only one who is involved in the improvement of the students. As compared to other stakeholders he rarely gets mentioned as a part of the success. But inside his mind, he knows that he contributes mainly to the change of attitudes, aptitudes, and the overall persona of the students. If one spends a little time in the placement facing the campus, he would certainly find that the trainer is the *only corner of comfort* for the students as the rest of the college, the principal, teaching, and the non-teaching staff are discussing the input quality and the shortcomings of the students.

A trainer can be very aptly compared with his equally ignored fellow countryman called a farmer. The Indian farmer is a special variety of human beings. Year after year, he is repeating a grueling schedule extending over ten months. Depending upon monsoon rains, a component which is unpredictable and erratic, combined with policies of the government, quality of seeds, acute shortages of funds, power, helping hands, and yet when the product is ready, he does not get the prices, or the credit both financial and moral. He is remembered only in the times of elections, and /or otherwise treated like a readymade material for ridicule. In the red-hot summer months of April and May, he toils for twelve to fourteen hours a day, with a **tremendous expectancy level** that everything would go right and unlike last year the coming season would be more productive. The same cycle continues for years. Something always goes wayward and he consoles his poor self by saying that next year would be better. Once he gets the better and bumper crop, he would marry his daughter or undertake the overdue repairs of his house or the yatra of the Chardham. He keeps his pursuit of the mirage of prosperity just like his father and grandfather. Even when he gets the bumper crop, he does not get the rates as they are controlled by people who care two hoots for the sheer unparalleled effort of the farmers. A farmer is rarely given the credit for the prosperity of the nation. He is remembered as a political necessity.

How does it relate to the trainers?

Let us see!

The trainer is the least glorified factor on campus. Never remembered for any sort of gratitude or felicitations. All such graces are reserved for the overbearing professors, principals, and governing body members.

He has no control over the students by way of internal marks or projects. The pomp and the limelight are mostly for the professors and faculty. Nothing wrong with it. The teachers have worked very hard to create a system like that. They (Teachers) manage to keep things in a way that is comfortable for them. They would get credit for everything and the criticism would be to the account of the trainer. They are busy in manipulating the loads, internals, evaluations and paid evaluations, external exams, and many such things as well as the routine gossip, so much so that they almost forget the *basic reason for their existence* in the college. The number of Ph.Ds.', the number of departments, the specializations, the principal, the labs, the sprawling *five-star* premises with swimming pools, tennis courts, and of course, the canteen gets mentioned in the brochures. Yes, *the number of placements* gets a prominent place in the information, but have you ever seen the name of the *placement officer* in any brochure? If you have seen such a brochure, consider the same as the exception and preserve it as a souvenir.

The Training and Placement Officer, TPO is responsible to place the students irrespective of their quality. He cannot talk about input quality or the ignorance of the students, even concerning domain knowledge. In the last year or the six months of the curriculum, he has to waive his magic wand and create a *super candidate* getting the best packages from the industry.

The whole process is as tiresome as agriculture farming in India. The trainer has no control and yet year after year, he is expected to produce silver-lined results. He has to tackle the internal heckling, as well as, he has to manage the very demanding external segment of corporates. When in a meeting with the management of the college *only one question keeps on ringing*. **A very stupid one, but it is there**.

How many companies would come to the college campus this year?

The management does not understand that the *smaller number of companies visiting the college* is ***better for the future*** *of the placement* scenario of the college. But no! They keep repeating the same. Worse is when they mention the other colleges in the area, without any rhyme or reason. They conveniently forget everything negative about their college, they support the faculty, despite the overall situation of the available teaching quality, the quality of the students, the depleted/defunct laboratories, the arrogant attitudes of the students, the non-cooperative staff, the shortage of funds, the resource crunch and many such important things. They just want HUNDRED PERCENT placements. So that they can get the next year's admissions and all-important money.

Coming back to ideal conditions the trainer is supposed to act as a matchmaker between the corporates and the candidates. So ideally, he should divide his work into two separate categories. First, he should ideally prepare all students for all possible questions in the interview, except for the industry-specific questions. In any case, the candidate would be required to address and answer some typical questions regarding himself. So, the preparations would be more or less similar, like the tilling of the farm. As soon as the crop is decided the requirements change. Similarly, as soon as the corporate is designated or identified, the needs change. The general approach includes the overall and common preparations, what is normally called personality development. Though many feel that personality is too big an aspect to be developed in such a short time. At best we can provide the students some markers, on which he has to work and continue for the rest of their life.

The trainer has to operate on multi-levels.

1. The first is to create a trust level. The students have many issues but they rarely open up with the correct people. If the students start discussing what they need and seek guidance from the trainer then he has begun in a great way. The field preparation before the seeds is sown can be compared with this. That he has a *place* and a *person* to go to is the basic purpose of the T&P cell.
2. The second step is to fortify the confidence of the students if they lack the same. To make him understand that he would not be the first human to face the campus placement process. There were many and there would be many. The second side of the coin of confidence is the overconfidence variety of students. The trainer has to cut their

aspirations, over expectations to size. The best way is to accept what he says and then ask him to justify the demands. A clear relationship between the qualifications, the industry norms, and the packages offered is to be established much before the actual grind starts.

3. The third step is to clarify the process of campus recruitment stepwise and bit by bit. There should be no confusion. The criteria like 60/65 / 70 and these days even 75 have to be explained. The numbers are the percentages for the tenth, twelfth, and seventh semesters in engineering or the case of MBA the graduation degree. Similarly, the weightage to the medium of education, family background, attempts taken for clearing the exams, English speaking, and writing should be clearly explained. Even better, the details should be mailed to each student, parent, and placement coordinator of the college. *Transparency is the keyword.* The student must be able to calculate his chances depending upon the selection criteria and if needed he must get guidance to improve his lots.
4. The fourth aspect is to explain that the recruitment process is more like a treasure hunt than a linear path. The first step has to be cleared before the student is allowed to compete in the next round.
5. The Fifth aspect is to explain the nature of competition. The competition is not with the outside students but with friends and batchmates. There should be no dilution in efforts and focus due to this. The trainer also has to always remember that the responsibility of creating interest and retaining focus lies squarely on him. The design and the delivery have to match the needs of the training programs. Also, the students are wary of the people like parents, teachers, seniors, peers, and neighbors who keep on repeating the need to study, concentrate, and focus. They just tell me to focus without actually telling me how to focus. The process of learning to focus and avoid distraction over some time is very vital. It helps to set time frames like 10 weeks, or 12 to follow a set routine which almost assures them of a good beginner job. They understand and are ready to stretch for a small span of time. The cost-benefit analysis of working right there as designed and needed, and the bright future waiting for them can do the basic shift in the attitude and the alignment. The students must understand the need to excel and how to excel without antagonizing the system and fellow students. The effort would need constant shepherding and motivation.
6. The sixth aspect is to make them aware of the possible failure in one or two placement drives. That a failure can also be a part of his life needs

to be explained. The trainer must explain that no success is automatic. It rarely helps to buckle down under the pressures of failures. 'You lose only when you feel that you have lost is what the trainer has to emphasize. Falling is no crime, but not getting up and trying again is a serious issue. The student before giving up must be aware that he is giving up a bright career, happy life, and recognition and submitting to a perceived failure. The industry averages must be discussed very openly. How many students clear the aptitude tests, and how many clear the further hurdles must be known to each and every student. They must know that it would not be the end of the world for them. The trainer needs to tell that there are only two classes in the business world. The first class tells others what to do and the other invariably does what it is told to. The difference between the two is huge and can lead to prolonged happiness or sorrow. A lot of things in the future life are directly connected to what a student does in the placement drive.

7. The trainer has to very essentially tell the students that he must complete each step of the process NOT as per his capacity but as per the norms set by the corporate. The concept of 'My best is not enough. Is it really the best?' has to be the guiding spirit.
8. The trainer needs to be a reliable partner and he must walk through the complete path with the student irrespective of his chances in the final race.
9. The trainer needs to know the types of training he is supposed to impart and the other issues that the students would encounter once they get selected. The trainer is more concerned with the types which help the students to get into the organizations, but at the same time, he should let his students know about the tougher variety. Let us see the types of training:

   i. **Induction training**: The students would begin their professional life with this type. His alertness is observed. It helps to have a session involving the details of the institution they studied so far. How much do they know?
   ii. **Internship training**: The students in the professional courses need to complete an internship program in one of the industries or companies they would like to work for. If he has seriously done this very essential aspect of his education, he would have lesser problems in getting merged into the culture and expectations of

the company. Sadly, very few give any due attention to SIP. Readymade SIP projects kill this aspect of the development of the students. This is an OJT type of training.

iii. **Apprenticeship training**: A student can get to learn exactly what he would be doing in the future in a company. He handles the machines, uses the software, interacts with labor, represents the company to the clients, maintains the accounts, and many such aspects. It is very near to a simulation exercise but the money he can earn for the organization is real. The major advantage to the student is that he is working under a supervisor who is responsible and accountable. Again, the seriousness with which the student undergoes this activity is reflected in his getting finally selected for the actual job in the same company. The offer letters tell us the story.

iv. **Job training**: More or less similar to the earlier ones, but is more specific. Such as specialized welding, or underwater repairs of structures. The more known term is the OJT (On- the- job training). The example of a floor supervisor who is less qualified but more adept and gives training to his would be superior. The trainee learns the value of humility and teamwork.

v. **Safety training**: One of the most neglected parts of educated human lives. For example, how many of us listen to the airline crew when they tell us about the masks and oxygen? Safety training is an aspect that can lead to better handling of unforeseen disasters in the plants, and accidents in the line of work. Artificial respiration, CPR, and first aid are now essential parts of knowledge.

vi. **Promotion training**: The training for promotions is very vital for the smooth assumption of charge by the promoted officer. In simple language, it means preparing a deserving person for the promotion. Enhanced line of command, area of operations, and more financial powers are some of the characteristics of this type of training.

vii. **Remedial training**: Over a period of time when an employee is working in a company, he may develop habits that inhibit him from discharging his duties. The training so designed to improve or correct the incorrect behavior of the employees is remedial training. It is a remedy for problems.

viii. **Retraining**: A company in the course of time expands, grows, diversifies, takes over some other companies, renovates, and adopts new technologies, so the employees need to be aligned to the newly charted course of the company. The old employees need to adapt and adopt the new culture and techniques to be successful in the new environment. If they receive proper Retraining, they would perform better. It helps the company in a great way as the other parameters for the older employees are already as per the needs. They can save a lot of time and resources as against the hiring of new employees.

10. **Avoid excess training**: The trainer and the TPO both have to pre-decide the extent of the training and the information provided to the placements aspiring students. In many cases, the students are overexposed to many unnecessary things which makes them disinterested in the entire activity of training. The excess of CV writing, communication, etiquette, grooming sessions, and how to even stand is very counter-productive. The trainer in the T&P department has to limit his efforts to facilitate the students to be able to get through the interview process. The trainer should NEVER assume the role of parents or the teachers as it leads to a certain disaster. He must remember that he cannot repair every wrong habit in the students inculcated due to poor parenting or poor teaching. The training should be ideally in limited steps and it should encourage the students to follow the same.

Ideally, the trainer should explain that many students before have followed the simple steps and have secured placements.

1. **The story of a rooster and a gem**: The fables have a great way to tell the essence of the process. The trainer must remember the story of a rooster who is not interested in the gem lying in the garbage heap.

There was a rooster looking for grains in the waste dump yard. There was a large red gem lying, which the rooster was constantly ignoring. It was useless for him as he could not eat the gem. The value of even a gem is with respect to who is looking at it.
Now there is nothing new in the story. We knew it and forgot along with many other gems. We were taught many things, invaluable at that, but we

rarely remember them. Further, very rarely do we actually use them. The students know that they have to stretch and that the effort put in now would make their future lives better or worse, but only a few change their present behavior. Not all! The trainer has to adjust to this fact.

Why?

As we grow older, we are tied up to a routine that makes us bored, and generally nonreceptive to new ideas. We know that an idea if rightly used can change our lives. But in the false momentum of life, we do not tend to stop and give the requisite time to the "life-changing" idea. The worst thing is we do not even have the inclination.

We blame everyone and everything except ourselves for our lots because we really do not give a damn about the gems we have and the gems we do not need. We spend time and energy running after the unwanted things and overlook what we have. What we have should make us happy. What we want generally, which does not belong to us, is a source of pain.

The management also overlooks the gems in the organization and wastes time looking for perceived gems in the competition firms.

In case the training activity begins in the final year or semester, in that short time, a customized and concentrated capsule has to be designed and imparted. But in rare cases where the managements are more proactive and progressive and they start the training process as early as in the first semester, the training activity can be very exhaustive as discussed in the chapter **Training for Placements Idea and Concept.** The students may be are very choosy and may have limited interest, but a good trainer who can connect creates a very good manager or entrepreneur.

The trainer has to understand that he is supposed to totally involve and improve each of the students to reach the desired final destination of an offer letter from the desired company. Performing with the available resources and then producing desired results is a serious business. Continuous stretching and then relaxing is a difficult and very exhausting task. The pain of not being able to participate in the actual process and producing results year after year is a real miracle and requires a strong philosophical base. The most admired and competent trainer, Yogeshwar Shrikrishna sat through the war without participating, but playing a major role in winning should never be forgotten. He motivated a loser and accompanied him throughout the process till he won the war. Similarly, when the students get the offer letters, the TPO can enjoy the gratification of seeing the success of placements. It is incomparable and it acts as a revitalizer for the next season.

The trainer must never forget that in spite of being trained and coached by the best in the world, the best content was delivered by the best in the best possible way to the best possible student, it took only ten days for Arjun, and that too in the constant company of Shrikrishna, to FORGET the training tenets. So, the trainer in the present mortal times that a certain part of the trainees would forget, perform badly, or fail altogether, and he must be prepared to take all such blows on his chin.

CHAPTER VIII

Final Semester Pangs.

Final Semester Pangs.

The life of any average student in India before he /she reaches the final semester of engineering or management is *full* of enjoyment, and if possible, *romance*. The journey is almost smooth and without any remarkable difficulty levels or hurdles. The college unduly helps him, in any which way, to reach the final lap by providing various *lifelines* like more deserving internal marks ATKT (allowed to keep term), Grace marks, attendance, and many such little things. So, before he reaches the final semester, he is either ready or more commonly not so ready, barring a few exceptions. Again, about life after finishing the curriculum either he is not aware or he does not care. He has a lot of unfounded ideas. So far, everything has somehow fallen into place without any significant contribution from his side, so he has a false sense of security and unqualified expectations from future employers, so much so, that he is sure that he is the chosen one by the almighty and would get a plum of a job just like it. Just like all other things in his life.

The environment around the student can be more conducive than what it is now. For various reasons the teachers, the administration, and the seniors avoid telling the student that he is not up to the required levels, or on the other side of the spectrum they just deflate him. Nobody wants to be the bearer of the unpleasant truth. Nobody asks the simple question, "Are you where you should be?". So, it is at the very last stage with all his prejudices he is thrown in front of the *wicked, and unforgiving* world. The people from the industry show him a proverbial mirror and he is shocked to see the "*real he or me* "as the case may be. He does not like what he sees. The stark difference between *the perceived me and the actual me* is heartbreaking. He is shattered and he is at the last tether of his rope when he finally realizes that he should go to the TPO. Not that he is very optimistic about the future nor he has any confidence that he can be altered or mentored to be the required specimen for the corporates.

Before the placement season, he never faced the facts of life. He was in his comfort bubble and he was sure that he was destined for the best in life. Just a few months before:

- Was he not the smartest kid?
- Was he not securing almost full marks?
- Was he not praised by one and all?

And then suddenly the moment of truth is in front of him in form of a rude rejection and he finds that he is not ready to accept that he is in any way responsible for the rejections he receives. He goes into a *blame-everyone mode*. Their parents, college, teachers, friends, peers, even the city, everything is responsible for his pathetic condition. Instead of accepting that he needs a basic shift and a change in his attitude or even a whole set of new attitudes, he tries to avoid, runs away from the facts, and finds himself in a depressing and dark hole. He is not reachable and does not want to share anything with anyone. The crisis of trust is complete, implicit, and absolute. **It is at this moment the only one person who can help him, who can tell him that not everything is lost,** that he can still bounce back, that six months from today he would be joking about his 'today', that there is a job waiting for him and it is just a matter of time before he would be leading a dignified and decent life, **is undoubtedly the TPO**. All others who were so important earlier and who mattered in his life have already condemned him as a failure. They have a look that says 'I told you so'. At that particular moment the student needs only support, and soothing company, and NOT the ever-present *Gyan*. He hates one and all, who discuss his problem rather than offering a viable solution. Even he contemplates suicide which is anyway a permanent solution to a temporary problem.

It is not easy for both of them. They form a very unlikely team of the unwilling student and the phlegmatic trainer. One is jittery, not in a listening mode, and very wary of any positive input and the other is in the knowledge of the complete process. It is up to the trainer to find a *common ground and communicate* for the best of the student. It has to be on a general level for the entire students and the other side a very personalized and even somewhat customized approach. Each student can be a test in itself but ultimately it works out as a unique reference story for future students.

One of the most hampering things is that the student whether in a prepared stage or an unfinished stage is ignorant about the future without a respectable job. The ignorance may be complete or partial but, in both cases, it hurts. To be without a job that too after a degree in engineering or management can be very difficult to sustain. One suffers a constant inquisition verbal or otherwise from the parents, relatives, peers, and anybody who has a semblance of a job. When in college one can escape to a relatively softer option of visiting the campus or the routine place of meeting friends. Now, one by one all my friends have got a job and they have migrated to their places of work. The vacuum is deadly and can weigh upon the mind of the unfortunate one who is still without a job. He knows that he would get a job but that knowledge is not enough to resist the prying glances. All the hard work put in for getting admitted to the college, and subsequent stretching during the tenure of the degree is reduced to **nil** and he is one of the most depressed human beings around. It is here the importance of a campus placement must be explained to the student. Getting a job through a campus placement process is easier as compared to later stressful hunting for a job. In the campus placements the students, the TPO, and the company are working towards placing the students whereas in the later process it becomes a difficult process as the company would like to first know why the student could not clear the campus placement.

The student caught in this web needs a steel frame for a mind and a rhino skin to tide over the most trying period of his life. Generally, he does not have and hence he suffers the most.

I think the trainer has to highlight this condition and its hopelessness to the aspiring student. He should guide and walk through the path with the student so that he does not fall into the proverbial pits and reach the destination. Even if all this guidance, counseling, and hand-holding do not motivate the student to put in his best effort for his good, then the student does not deserve the break. He would be an insignificant part of the workforce instead of the management, and he would be *taking orders instead of giving them*. Once, he misses the campus placement train, he would always lag and lead a very painful and full of regrets life. The trainer has to explain that there is a very **marginal difference between the selected and not selected while the student is still in college,** and he would help the student to bridge the gap in a matter of time and effort.

The beginning of the pangs sets in pretty silently and is realized later, only when the pain level increases. The fact hits the student that he is at the last leg of education and he may not have the cushion he was used to so much. That he would have nothing to do worthwhile if he remains jobless is a depressing feeling and he has a trailer of his life when he misses the campus placement bus, in the first one or two placement drives. The sudden knowledge that whatever he knows so far is not enough or properly aligned to succeed in the placement drive, is a sinking feeling. He does not have a readymade ***go-to*** person due to the peculiar structure of the education system. People seem to avoid him. That it is the same routine that is faced by almost all is not noted by his mind. Those very successful people and those who come and tell success stories in the alumni meets also had to face rejection, which is lost upon him. The fear of perceived ridicule takes over and he faces a paralysis of thoughts and processes.

One full session of **potential analysis and about immediate job opportunities** with the TPO should be enough for his recovery and that is what the trainer must attempt to do. If one session is not enough, there should be two or three, but the student must be made to realize that he is undergoing a *routine* process, which has rejection as a major component. That *he still* ***possesses all the qualities he had before his rejection***. It is like Virat Kohli losing his form temporarily. It is just a matter of time before the jigsaw puzzle would be completed. The example of the jigsaw puzzle is very apt because every puzzle *gets completed*, some take more than usual time but, in the end, it is *always completed*. Similarly, every normal, and sane student would get a job.

To avoid the last-minute stress and very painful analysis of the things that went wrong, or thinking about how they could have been avoided the student needs to keep following things in the uppermost crest of his mind and focus on things that would fetch him the placement.

1. **Too much importance** is attached to the Grades/ CGPA/ internal marks/practical exams/ projects and all routine activities which are the part and parcel of integrated courses like engineering or management. A student with a 9.9 CGPA is welcome but only if he has some other complementary skills. He should be healthy, pleasant and appear as a team man. 'Is he able to comprehend and apply his theoretical knowledge to some practical application', would be a million-dollar question, he needs to answer. Can he at least recall the relevant chapter when he needs to solve a problem in the field? Good academics can assure you an interview call but unless you become a complete package, as they say, you would rarely get the job you want. Each student has to develop his scale and proportion about how much he needs to give weightage to academic grades and other desirable qualities in himself to get a job. Nobody would suggest completely ignoring the CGPA but the student must not neglect the other components like current news awareness, General Knowledge, certifications in software or courses like

AutoCAD, communication skills, certification in foreign languages, and many such small things which together would present him as a desirable and complete person.

2. **Poor Communication skills**. - The placement-seeking student in the various courses must check out the statistics available about what is the percentage of students who get a job. The AICTE, UGC, and various other agencies have published papers with very disheartening numbers. In the engineering stream, they say that only about ten to fifteen percent of students are employable. The further dampener is that this number includes premier institutes like IIT, NIT, BITS, and some other upcoming names. So, in reality, it means that only about five to seven percent of private institutes are employable. Everybody knows this simple fact and yet anybody, who matters, feels that somebody would do something and **nobody does anything**. The management instead of investing so much in non-living infrastructures, and employing overpaid professors with doctorates, should put the appropriate effort into the students and their overall development. Right from the first semester a suitable induction training schedule must be designed and followed.

One of the major issues is the communication problem. It is surprising but it exists in various degrees in various students. What you are supposed to know, what you know, how much you have understood, and how much of what you have understood can be expressed in a convincing fashion matters a lot more. **That you know something and are unable to express hurts even more than being ignorant**. There is a direct relationship between the salaries offered and communication abilities. The student with better expression would be offered a job. The art of saying things in an acceptable and pleasant way is the top-drawer skill every aspiring student must have.

3 **Avoid Rote learning**: - Most students believe in last-minute studies just for the sake of xeroxing the same in the answer sheets to pass the exams. It may help, but it has a limited value. Rote learning is defined in Google as the '*Mechanical or habitual repetition of something to be learned*. (In India, we call it *ratta marna*.) The student forgets that he needs to undergo the complete process of learning and writing to be able to convert himself into something called a professional. He should not and cannot pick and choose. Professional courses should not be treated as buffet dinners. **Comprehension is a must.** The more he understands the topic, the lesser he would have to remember the same. The students have to understand

that if he prepares for forty percent passing grades, they cannot expect to have the luxuries of life. He must not expect a hundred percent from his future life. He would lead a life full of compromises and deficiencies. He would remember every unwanted shortcut he took during his college life throughout his life.

1. **Undermining the internship**: - The students tend to undermine the importance of the internship during the tenure of the course. Most stupid students waste the time. The internship in its various formats ensures that the student gets exposure to the very environment he is supposed to spend his entire life. He gets to work, with experienced people, and gets a huge amount of practical knowledge through the industry grapevine, he becomes a part of the process where the theory is converted into practice and revenue is generated. If he misses this golden chance, he would spend a huge period learning during his employment. The internship is like the simulated jigs or planes where you tend to learn much more without any risk. You are making mistakes and still learning the invaluable tricks of the trade. There is very little accountability as you are under the wings of your industry guides.
2. **Industrial projects**: - The students feel that industrial project is not very important. They can manipulate. They are very wrong. Projects whether industrial or academic can have a great effect. They can convert an ordinary student into something more useful and worthwhile. The actual application of what he has learned teaches him much more than he could ever imagine. The coordination of the various resources and the much-needed cooperation of the team, the adjustments, the adoption of the innovations, and the techniques needed to accomplish the given task can together teach the students how to get things done without antagonizing their superiors and colleagues. The taste of success once tasted can remain forever and would be a great booster to the sagging confidence if needed in the future. *That I can do anything* is the strongest tonic for young managers.
3. **The new techniques**: - One of my friends who is a senior director in a multinational software company always says that people must keep abreast with new technologies. He told me that the new things are with a very short shelf life and they keep on changing very fast. *For the* engineers and managers, it is not just enough that they should be aware but quick enough to master them and exploit them to their advantage.

Big data analytics, AI artificial intelligence, machine learning, design thinking certification, advanced communication techniques, and digitalization are some things young people must be aware of. The point is that all these are in addition to the already present software Languages, AutoCAD, space dynamics, etc.

4. **Internet savvy**: - The world is expanding but mostly only on a virtual scale. A person without internet expertise is likely to lag. One must understand that the internet gives the information literally at the fingertips, at practically no or negligible cost, without any fuss, without any time limits (It is available 24x7) and nobody gets wise about your shortfalls. The information is simply huge and it is up to the student to pick and choose and get world-class experts to talk to him through YouTube, blogs, or essays. Even in Geeta, there is a shloka that talks about the relationship between available knowledge and the capacity of a person to absorb. Yogeshwar Shrikrishna compares knowledge with a big lake full of sweet water and the seeker of knowledge with a thirsty traveler. The traveler can drink only a little water, though the lake has much more to quench the thirst of many. The student knows what can be good, what can be useless for his thirst, and what quantity is essential. Social media though condemned by many can help the student if he joins the right groups and get a fair share of peer and expert learning. The new trends, the new technology, and the new ways of looking at the same things can be learned.
5. **Stupid cliché:** - When the student is in his final year, he feels that he has achieved a great deal of knowledge. He is attracted by concepts like atheism, socialism, and many such irrelevant and unnecessary things. They can be termed as distractions, and he must not get diverted. Those things *do not* matter. All *isms like socialism, communism, and others* have limited significance in his present life and a timeframe. What matters during the placement time is whether he can raise his standards to the requisite level to become a successful employee or an entrepreneur.
6. **What you "can"**: When you begin, to do, what you are told by your trainers, you are in for a lot of surprises. What you thought you would find and what you actually find can be very different. The amount of time you take to adjust, learn, and then acceptably deliver the same can be the difference between the average, good, and best practicing managers in the future.

   The sync between, **what you *"can"*, what you *"want"* and what you** "***like***" is of paramount importance for you. Doing is the best belief-building measure, student once knows the same can never be the same old mediocre one. He learns, perceives, plans, and produces the best.

The pangs are defined as sudden physical pain or a strong emotion creating turmoil inside. The entire effort on the part of the trainer needs to create awareness about what can go wrong and how to prevent it by some simple tricks and what is available on the platter if the student manages to get placed. The disturbances are mostly temporary and topical and most have sustained the same. The mother undergoes the worst and almost impossible pain, she is yelling, almost becoming hysteric, but all the pain is gone the moment she holds her newborn baby, her best creation so far. She forgets all pain, and discomfort of nine months of pregnancy and is rightly filled with love and pride. Similarly, when the student gets his offer letter, he **forgets** all the pain, ridicule, toiling, and stretching beyond limits and he is just filled with relief, pride, and joy.

***

CHAPTER IX

Mentoring in Training For Placements

Mentoring in Training For Placements

The concept of mentoring is not new to Sanatan Indian people. The Gurukul concept was mainly based on this principle. The student was just about eight or nine years when he was admitted to a gurukul far from his residence and parents. The Guru was the main sculptor who had a unique mixture of textbook learning, extra-curricular activities, social relationships, competing with the best around them, and aptitude development for each of his disciples. It was a long association of about twelve years (also known as a Tapa), and the education was compared with Tapasya or penance. Just imagine the amount of mentoring that must have gone into the development of each student, and the happiness of the Guru at the end of the same. Along with many other things and concepts the concept of mentoring was also lost by the Indians. Reasons are many and often repeated so we do not go into them.

The main difference between those days and the present activity of training for placements activity is the age difference. Those students were young and very ready for getting moulded by their gurus. They were teachable, trainable, malleable and most importantly willing to listen to the Guru. Their slate was clean. They had no prejudices, no premonitions, no false ideas of esteems and that is why they both were successful. Come to the present day lots of students and one is in for a shock. The students in engineering are in their late teens, but their opinions are quite strong. Also, due to their peculiar relationship with their teachers, they have no faith in the systems that they are supposed to follow. They have many unofficial sources of information, which in most cases, is the main reason for the below-par performance of these students. Lack of belief and crisis of trust haunt them. They do not believe that they can improve and get the job they want if they follow certain simple routines laid down by the TPO. So, they follow the path of degrading the system, ignoring the T&P cell circulars, not preparing for the aptitude tests and many of them have no idea about why they fail the simple interviews.

In the case of MBAs, they are slightly elder, they have graduated, but very rarely do they live up to the expectations of the TPO. They share their basic problems with all other fellow stream students. Lack of communication, lack of content, lack of soft skills, lack of confidence, lack of self-respect and many such shortcomings are commonly found in students who are aspiring for jobs. The only common thing is that they all want fat salaries and that they want to enjoy their lives.

On this background, the process of mentoring becomes extremely important for the TPO and the students. Mentoring mainly includes changing the mindsets from minus ten to zero, to begin with, and later on, convincing them that they can somehow change themselves into something more presentable and get the jobs.

One more serious problem with the TPO is that he does not get enough time and hold over the students. Reason one is that the students do not understand the importance of employability skills. On average, a TPO has to spend about four hours individually with each student. This is in addition to the combined sessions of placement training. Roughly it would be like as below:

- 25 minutes on his resume
- 35 minutes on his aptitude tests results
- 45 minutes on his GD participation
- 60 minutes for his mock interviews
- 90 minutes for his counselling and queries

And after this, he has to find time to mentor the students or he has to alternately find suitable and willing staff members who would walk that extra yard needed when you mentor the students.

Classically, mentoring is defined as teaching, training, and /or coaching someone younger over a period of time to accomplish a certain task.

They say that you need not get involved in your job and you should be able to distance yourself from the work pressures of your job. If you are working in mentoring you must immediately forget the above. The mentor has to be involved, has to work overtime, and feels the pain of failure as intensely as the student and yet on the surface, he should not show any signs of weakness. Once a mentor always a mentor, means that this is a lifelong and 24x7 job. He also should be ready to distance himself from the student once the student gets the job as there would be many pouncing for getting the credit. The mentor has to be a *sthitpragya*. The mentor needs to silently smile at such people. Mentoring is a back-office activity, very important but would never be in the limelight.

Types of mentoring the TPO can choose from:

A. Informal mentoring: When the relationship is less business-like, not bound by definite timelines, and not aiming for a goal in a specific time the mentor can advise over a long period of time. There can be many rehearsals, and many attempts, but in last the mentee turns out perfect.

1. The mentor and mentee select rather than appoint each other.
2. They are both ready to spend a long time together, many times even a lifelong association.
3. The outcome of the association is not very crystal clear. It is fluid and flexible. It is not pre-decided.
4. The access is limited to one person each, very rarely two. It is an exclusive possession type in a positive way.
5. The outcomes

Examples of such mentoring are in classical Indian music. It is said that Pandit Bhimsen Joshi was singing "*Sa*" for nearly ten years before he was allowed to proceed further. Maybe, it is a fable. But when he started performing, he became the best in the business of vocal music for decades. There would be many others.

A. Formal Mentoring: This type is mainly connected with the official corporate world, which is essentially driven by pre-decided goals and objectives.

1. The goals are pre-decided by the organization in consultation with the mentor.
2. The results are monitored and measured.
3. Access is not restricted, but depending upon the situations and the resources available more people can be admitted to the programme.
4. The program is run by an individual or a group of experts in the company.
5. The support mechanism is in place by way of additional expert inputs, and scrutiny by outside experts.

The process of mentoring: Understanding the process of mentoring is very vital for the mentor. The process can be customised to suit specific requirements, but generally, the mentoring process would have the following steps. The sequence may vary but the process would be similar.

1. Introduction: The mentee and the mentor need to know each other really well. Inside out as they call it. This is very much like the pre-treatment of components of many processes in the industry. The trust-building begins here. They both should know the basic reason for their future association and the estimated outcome. The tone of the things to come in the future is set here. The belief that the mentor is capable enough and the mentee is receptive enough should be checked here.
2. The foundation: The roles of both the mentee and the mentor should be defined at least on a broad scale if not specific. The same change as per the needs but the final outcome should be unchanged. There should be mutual acceptance of the roles assigned.
3. Proper orientation: The mentee needs to be in a proper state of mind so as to achieve the purpose of the mentoring programme. This is accomplished by having a properly designed orientation capsule. It should reduce the tensions which would be caused due to misunderstanding and retain the motivation till the purpose is achieved.
4. Collaboration and cooperation: The mentor and the mentee have to work together. The mentee must feel that he is also a vital part of the process almost like an equal partner rather than a docile worker carrying out the instruction. The mentee needs to understand the team and its power.
5. The SWOT analysis: Here the mentor needs to discuss and dissect the pluses and minuses of the student. He has to explain the worth of the assets and the potential dangers of the perceived liabilities. Expected problems need to be seen and possible solutions need to be found after the discussion with the mentee. When the mentee finds out that he can participate and even find solutions to his so-far impossible problems his confidence is boosted many times. The mentor has to explain that the mentee would be immensely benefitted if he does a SWOT analysis on two different levels. One for the public, (*as in the safe mode* in the computers) and the other for personal which is the real one and which can actually help him in future improvement and development.
6. The personal and the professional profiles or also called outlines: The mentor has to take lead and get the mentee to draw a personal picture

of himself *as of today* and *after the completion* of the mentorship programme. The mentor has to actually give the mentee a chart for this purpose. This exercise also throws some light on the expectations, which can be altered as per the needs of the organization. The professional profile of the mentee can be the roadmap. What he thinks he would be after the mentoring has to be actually put on paper and preserved.

7. Period of transition: This can be less or more depending upon the capability of the mentee, the difficulty levels of the task, his overall ability to work with the team, his dedication, and his ability to put theory into finding solutions in practical situations. For the first time, he is doing something solely by himself. He either relishes the same or he perishes. He works independently, **but in a controlled environment.**

Benefits of a well-organized mentoring programme. The benefits can be many but a few are mentioned below:

1. **Career guidance or counselling**: The mentor has to utilise the opportunity to further the cause of the programme. A better-counselled student or employee can be better handled. His idea of the future would be clear. He would ideally know what to expect and even more importantly how to overcome the issues.
2. **Practical training or even the OJT**: Mentoring can prepare him for the training. The gap between the theory and the actual application without any fumble can be a major asset of the OJT. We all know that one minute with the shift supervisor in a factory can be more than many sessions in college. Learning about the tricks of the trade is the biggest benefit. If the mentee is in marketing, he would know about the most important aspect of marketing which is *handling of objections.*
3. **Sharing of information/knowledge**: Each industry has a specific intelligence quotient which needs to be shared. Mentoring sessions can be one of the best ways to impart such knowledge along with the pride to belong to such a great organization. Here the mentee undergoes a major shift from Basic knowledge to specific knowledge which makes him competent and experienced. The first-hand transfer of specific knowledge from the experts without any dilution can be magical.
4. **The induction of the employee**: One of the most important things in the better performance of the incoming employee is his proper induction into the organization. well begun is half done is very true. What he

learns from a mentor is again a concentrated dose of only those things which are good for him and for the organization. The elimination of unnecessary things makes things simple and doable. The best induction is in the army and probably the longest lasting. Even after retirement, the army person is as he was in the service. The mentoring helps ease the setting of new people in the already smoothly running machine.

5. **Understanding the culture and the mission**: The mentor can be a great help in creating the right impression about the company or the mission like placements. A dedicated person to make the mentee understand what is acceptable and what is taboo in the company is very vital. A mentor can make him understand the values, culture, and methods of operations in the company without any obvious antagonism and embarrassment of public exposure. Once understood the mentee can easily follow the route.
6. **Leadership skills searching and developing**: We all know that a real leader is as rare as a black pearl. A sensible approach to leadership development is through proper mentoring. The mentor is equipped to spot the raw talent which can be later polished and developed. The simulation techniques used by the mentor can be very productive as the mentee is leading in almost a real situation. The attitude and the aptitude to volunteer for leadership is discovered by the mentor at an early stage. There are many methods, and the experience tells the mentor which is to be used for which mentee.
7. **Retention of employees**: One of the biggest problems faced by HR department people is attrition. Mentoring as against regular classroom training has an edge. One-to-one mentored people have better chances to stick around for more time, however, a detailed study is suggested. Mentoring is a comprehensive process including teaching, training, creating an atmosphere that is more conducive to learning, fostering relationships, can provide role models, can create reasons to look forward. The mentee is clear about what he is supposed to do and what would be his rewards or awards. Retention is a typical process which is mostly mishandled by companies. The HR staff fails to provide reasons to stick around. That is a separate issue. The study of exit interviews is rarely given the importance it deserves. No employee would want to leave a company unless extreme reasons force him to. The clarity is provided by the mentors.

Designing a successful mentoring programme: Is there any fool-proof way to conduct a mentoring programme? No is the simple answer. The why is also simple. Mentoring involves people of various mental ages and mental abilities and hence it is very difficult to generalise. If it could be done the first casualty would be the mentoring programme itself.

1. The First step is to crystallise the exact WHY for the mentoring programme. The slimmer the objective is the better the chances for success. More words in the objective are more confusing which leads to failure. If the **why** is clear the **how** usually follows right.
2. The process from point A to point Z needs to be clear in the minds of the mentee and his mentor. The amount of hard work in any project in the modern days is immense and the pain doubles if it does not meet with the desired success. So, it helps to know the roles, who controls and why. The coordination has to be finetuned and all stakeholders should head for the same destination and that too in tandem.
3. The leader: There is a sense of false security in the presence of the immense data we have these days. The data by itself is as good as a book in the library not read by many. There is something more complex than the simple data and execution of the orders which is provided by the able leader. To accomplish something spectacular with the available resources is possible only when the process is handled, supervised, corrected midway and providing encouragement to the weakest link in the chain. Many things that seemed impossible were and are achieved by the sheer passion of the leader. The desired approach by the leader or the manager is fair to all and focused only on the goals.
4. Overall supervision: Any project, more so when there is a strong human element involved needs constant supervision to keep the project on track. Cajoling, coaxing, and even coercing when needed have to be used. Also, the availability of the right tools and equipment matters a lot. Any tool that saves time and also manages to transfer the message to many more than one-to-one is needed.
5. What do I have in it? The question keeps on propping very irritatingly. The mentor and the manager have to answer this very often and with some basic consistency. More fashionably it is called a *win-win* situation. Maintaining it requires exceptional people to handle the ongoing process.

6. Rethink, and even redesign if needed: The midcourse corrections should be included as a necessary part and parcel of the process. There is no shame in changing the course, person or even a process if it succeeds in the end. But you have to be very fair and open about the same. The rule is to inspect, measure, course correct, listen to people and include any positive suggestions. Brilliance can be random and it still shines the same irrespective of its origin. As a lion does, the leader has to keep looking back, check-up whether the team is on the track and must ensure that the team is not lost.
7. Mentoring is a part of management word. Management can be broken down into three words. Man+Age+Ment. It can be expanded as a man coming of age by mentoring. Mentoring begins from the first day of human life and ideally continues till the end.

CHAPTER X

Role of Microsoft Excel in Placements.

Role of Microsoft Excel in Placements.

The first thing the TPO must check is his knowledge and expertise in Microsoft Excel. It is not enough to just be aware; he should be equipped to process the data as per the demands of the corporates and his ever-anxious management. If he is dependent on somebody, then *that somebody* would be a major threat to him in the long run. He should be ready to answer the queries on a 24x7 basis. The better the TPO is in Microsoft Excel activity, the better his results as a TPO.

Complete data about the students in an excel format is his best ally in the next six months of the placements season. So, he must deliberate, discuss, design, and develop the best way to present his data to the management and the corporates. There is no thumb rule, but some basic and general things must be included and then the specific details added as per the situation's demand.

Matching the list of students with what the company desires are the major reason why the data needs to be in Excel. Maybe there are some more options but this works nicely. One or two sample formats can be found on the net. But please note that they are not the best or most comprehensive. They may not suit the specific requirement of the institute. The TPO has to use his inputs and the *local intelligence* to improve or even he must make his own. The world-famous *cut copy and paste* rarely help.

At the beginning of the season, the pace is slow, one can manage with some sluggish or incomplete data, but as the momentum of the process gathers as the season sets in, the time is less, and requirements are always urgent and almost instant. That time the only thing that helps the TPO is his laptop and the excel sheets inside. If this is up to date, he can cater to the needs of the corporates in a minute and send the relevant data.

The students in the data sheet have to be contacted, informed, and followed up which is possible only if your data is up-to-date, correct, and comprehensive.

The sheet also helps the TPO in the meetings with the management, and that too with facts and figures. The TPO learns very fast that his opinions do not matter at least in the beginning, so he should have supporting facts and figures.

One of my very senior friends in this T&P activity says "At the beginning of my stint I always felt like the traditional bahu in the orthodox family. Everyone had a look and an opinion reserved for me. It was very trying but now I have got the control". There is a lot of sense in this statement.

Segregation of the students based on:

- Name
- Age
- Sex
- Educational qualifications
- Grades so far
- Patents
- Summer Internship
- Other volunteering assignments
- Gradation of college
- Specializations
- Residence
- Language abilities
- Attempts for clearing the exams
- Medium of instruction
- Certifications
- Extra-curricular activities
- Paper publications
- Projects
- Physical attributes like height, weight, etc
- Hobbies
- Special interests
- And information about so many other aspects which are demanded by the companies.

The TPO needs to learn some functions in Excel such as the following

1. VLOOKUP
2. PIVOT Table
3. Conditional formatting
4. IF statements

5. And he should be very I repeat very conversant with all formulae in excel etc.

The combination of real data and the application of Excel or ERP can make the life of a TPO a bit more comfortable. All this is at the tip of your little finger and instantly, which makes you more confident and efficient.

So, it helps the TPO to excel in Excel!

CHAPTER XI

Proposed Placement Process

Proposed Placement Process

The placement process has two main components. The Supply and Demand of the placement activity form the process. The first includes preparing the students for the placements which are covered under the training activity, while the second is getting the exact requirements from the companies

The Supply Aspect

The supply aspect is handled by the institution, and it has a set pattern that needs to be completed well before the placement season starts. The relevant and updated information of the student's needs to be ready and must be communicated to the willing corporates at the flick of the computer. For this the steps are as follows:

Step 1: Database

- In the preparation of the general database, every institution has this data from the admissions. The better classification at the data collection step usually helps the T&P.

- In Engineering colleges, the data becomes significant from the third year whereas in MBA colleges; the information about the basic qualifications plays an important role.

- The profile of each student in an Excel format is a must.

The formats can be as per the customized needs but they must have full details. A format is attached but you can always improve upon the same.

- Any relevant additional information must be sent to the T&P on a periodical basis. All achievements of the students *if reported* properly and on time help to get better placements.

Step 2 Analysis of the data

- Students per specialization
- Language abilities
- Sex ratio (Boys and Girls) per college and specialization.
- Percentages
- Achievements like national debates, the publication of papers, internships, stipend amounts, contributions to social causes, and such activities.

Step2 **B** --The data in the case of the management, and pharmacy colleges can be based on the stream, percentages so far, sector choices, and any other specific requirement of the corporate.

Step 3 Pre-placement Interviews or Mock interviews

- **Pre-placement interviews form one of the most important steps.**

It is the first interaction between the T&P and the students. The students (with their practical or impractical ideas) have to understand what the industry wants. The students need to do a serious cross-check and need to adjust according to what is expected by the industry. The T&P here has to be ruthless and they have to be a real representative of the corporates. It always helps to have some teachers on the interview panels which prevents future clashes.

- This helps the T&P cell to segregate the students. The segregation is mainly for the ready-to-market and not yet-finished goods.
- This also helps in the identification of the training needs. Separate students have separate needs, but a group can be formed to facilitate the easy transfer of knowledge, and test it in a limited period.
- The students are made aware of what they want and what they are likely to get. The trick here is never limiting the expectation of the student but making him ready for the same from an industry point of view.
- The history of the placements, earlier students' satisfaction, and the stability factors are explained to the students so that a clear and transparent understanding is achieved.
- Assignments are given to the students depending on their sector choices and it is imperative on the part of the students to submit the same on time. It is seen that only those who start right finish.

- The students are taught about how to present their assignments, projects, and achievements and further put to test shortly.
- If handled properly the students get to know the seriousness of the T&P process.

Step 4 Sector-Specific Assignments

- Depending upon the generation of the students would be given assignments that would be sector and company-specific. It has been seen that when the students appear for the interview with specific reports have better chances of competing and clearing.
- Presentations of such reports are a great help.

Step 5 Co-operation from the respective college and faculties.

- Though the responsibility of the placements is squarely on the T&P cell, it is not possible to work in isolation. The teachers are a big influence and rightly so. **T&P can succeed only if there is harmony between academics and T&P.**
- Teachers should help with specific training.
- Teachers in the third and fourth years should align their teaching to the needs of the placement. Their assignments should help the students to understand the application of the concepts in the industry.

The Demand Aspect.

Simultaneously with the preparation of the supply, t T&P cell should start to look for the following aspects.

- Identification of growth sectors
- Expansion possibilities
- GDP LINKAGE with possible placements
- Placement history
- Alumni satisfaction

Step1 Approaches

- Through existing Data bank
- Through the references of top management

- Through the references of teachers
- Through the references of students
- Through the references of the alumni
- Generation through T& team

Step2 Listing

- List of probable companies
- Contacts
- Process
- Analysis of the process
- Results
- Getting Appointment letters.

Step 3Understanding Corporate Culture

- Most standard companies have their categories of campuses.
- They value the actual application of the concepts
- Any practical experience is valued.
- **They want students with the right attitude rather than percentages.**
- They have set processes for selections; they rarely accept deviations.
- It is better to approach the national companies than the local enterprises.
- If our institutions are not up to per their present evaluations then we have to work harder and get upgraded as per their norms.
- They prefer the staying students.
- They want long-term relations.
- They are ready to pay more but after some time. The students have to understand this simple fact.

Step 4Rules and Regulations

- The placement activity is about **assistance rather than a guarantee**.
- Procedures for nominations
- Screening of nominations
- The ratio of the company to students
- **Multiple offer letters are very dangerous. This single aspect kills the placement process over some time.**
- Categories of placement based on quality

Many things take time and it is not in the control of the T&P cell however it helps to be ready, keep reviewing and be patient. *Keep doing the right things believing the right results are just around the corner.* The process involves many heterogeneous factors, many of which are very subjective in nature. But the joy of placing our students in good companies with good packages overrides all such problems. The sense of gratification received by the final placements and the knowledge that we have somehow impacted the lives of many young students acts as a catalyst for the remaining time.

***

CHAPTER XII

SKILL DEVELOPMENT (LOCAL & GLOBAL)

SKILL DEVELOPMENT (LOCAL & GLOBAL)

Before we go into the details let us first understand the terms involved. Let us know what is a skill, development, and global.

The skill is defined as the ease with which one performs a specific job. The Merriam-Webster defines skill as

1a): the ability to use one's knowledge effectively and readily in execution or performance. b: dexterity or coordination especially in the execution of learned physical tasks.

And

2: a learned power of doing something competently: a developed aptitude or ability language skills.

Development: Generally, when people talk about development, they mean growth. Development does have growth as one component but it is different from growth.

Development is generally discussed **for the absence of** it, in most cases, at a very painful post-mortem meeting. To be a developed person, the person has to understand that he is not developed as of date. Why development is needed? One line answer to this is **"He who stops being better, stops being good"** Development is a constant urge to be better and hence should be an ever-present phenomenon in every aspect of human life. Changing for the better and getting evolved is development. The development **is growing towards a pre-planned goal**. It is a journey towards becoming the best in the business. In the language of physics, it is a vector function rather than a scalar. The vector function has magnitude and necessarily moves toward a particular direction. In management, the development has to be a pre-decided function. In a very dynamic scenario of commerce today, where a technology by itself can be obsolete in a short period and hence discarded, the aspect of development can be of vital importance.

Global: The concept of globalization is quite new. Earlier humans had no idea of anything so big as a globe as they had a limited vision. In the last century, the concept of being global was limited to some trade activity and world wars. The global term achieved its significance when the concept of the internet was launched. More specifically the digital platforms. Communication became faster beyond any comprehension. The instant access to anyone anywhere in the world or even in space started the concept of being global. Global means *across the globe or concerning the whole world.*

The entire perspective of looking at anything changed after the concept of global came into being. It is mainly very significant for the information and its flow. As well as for goods where the market has no limit. A small-town handicraft manufacturer can sell his products globally. Because of the surging demand, the spread of the internet, the platforms like WhatsApp, Facebook, YouTube, and zoom, the requirement for skilled people is on the rise globally. The five factors of people, planet, peace, partnership, and prosperity would lead the world. When one starts thinking for people across the world, he takes the first step towards thinking globally.

A person is born with some talents that we find in our daily routine. We say he has it in his blood. So, does it mean that only those things can be further developed? Or everyone can be trained in everything? Yes, that is the answer. The problem would be in how many months or years? There has to be a calculation of the cost involved and the benefits perceived if a person is to be trained. Moreover, all this activity has to be voluntary. The person to be successful in training has to be willing to undergo the pain, stress, and grind. He needs to be clear about the positive changes in him to move ahead in the race called life.

Let us find out if there is any **difference between skill and talent**.

A talent is inherited from the parents. For example, a Lata Mangeshkar is born with a golden voice, blessed by a tremendous ability to learn the intricacies of classical music, and then trained to sing a mindboggling number of songs in ten different languages. A Kapil Dev is born with cricket, a Sehwag with an inborn gift of hand-eye coordination, and then faces the ruthless world but reaches the top. Ali Sher, a caddy born with talent and then some passion becomes the Golf champion. Sadly, all talent does not always reach the logical end because of various other factors needed for success.

During my research for the book, I was pleasantly surprised that governments all over the world have become more concerned about the shortage of skilled workforce. A detailed paper "*A Skilled Workforce for Strong, Sustainable and Balanced Growth*" published by the ILO gives a rare insight into the issue and steps taken to resolve the issue globally. Talent is the primer needed to learn the skills. The person with talent is trained more easily than the person without the talent, aptitude, and willingness to learn. The teachability of a person can be the difference between the result and the failure of a training program.

The idea of training whether in the industry or institution is simple. Finding out the innate abilities of a person in question, then identifying persons with similar abilities, aligning them with the skill requirements of the jobs. The HR manager or the TPO would be immensely benefitted if he has the checklist ready job-wise or company-wise. Suppose, you need a person for customer services then there must be a list with which the talents of a person or the learned skills through a course have to be tallied. The more the right ticks mean more chances for the success of the person. The basic need for successful training is the talent pool search. The person with the inborn talent needs only the training and the inculcation of the discipline to be a star. The problem with talent is that the pain of the application is rarely understood. The consistency factor is forgotten by talented people. Doing anything like cooking, sports, coding, or writing articles, for the sake of entertainment and pursuing the same as a career are two different things. The TPO must make his students understand the difference between a pastime, hobby, special interest, and passion for future clarity. Let us find out what it means.

Cooking as a hobby once in a while and becoming a chef serving a thousand people are not the same. Thousand people with different choices and tastes need a great understanding of food, quantity, timing, cuisine, and multitasking as the period for breakfast, lunch, or dinner is restricted. The diverse activities needed to be mastered by the chef and then perform at top performance levels for weeks, months and years do need stiff training.

Writing one software program is not enough. As a developer, you need to write programs and create codes daily. In addition, you always have unrealistic deadlines. The pressures of a release and the constantly changing demands of the client make the development which is not as rosy as it seemed in my college days. The TPO must make all software aspirants seat in one place for ten hours and work with the PC. That can be the best initial training. It can be a great test of combating unnecessary restlessness of young students.

Writing an article for the college annual is good but it is not what a sub-editor or the scriptwriter does. The sub-editor writes daily at least three or four pieces on topics he never heard of. The creative ability of a writer and what is needed as a professional columnist or editor are different.

When we see a Sachin or a Kapil, their best is on the show. The tip of the iceberg does not show the efforts below the surface levels. It does not show how they must have fought the failures, overcome their frustrations, and tackled the faulty systems which at times almost put a full stop to their careers. We tend to forget the mad effort of these legends. The number of hours in the net, the number of balls bowled or faced, the stiff attitude of the coaches, the ridicule of the neighbors, the indifferent attitude of Indian sports management, and the very erratic responses of the crowd, we tend to forget. Facing all these hurdles, they performed for years, and yet after one single failure, their houses are pelted with stones and even burned. Their Twitter/ WhatsApp is full of hate mail.

So, it is difficult to excel, even when you have talent, but without talents, it becomes *highly improbable if not impossible.* Many superb talents were wasted and many skills never saw the stage of success. For being on the Olympic medal podium, that too just for a minute or so the player usually had put in years of total rigorous practice. Many burst, into tears, when they are on the stage because they feel the pain.

The company has its product, process, and person-centric programs for its employees. The whole purpose of talent acquisition is to match the skill sets of a person with those required at the workplace. When they hire an experienced person, they can dig a little more into the background and the experience of the candidate. But in the case of the freshers, the corporates have to spend more time, money, and other resources. There is a scheme called a *continuous education program* which ultimately results in a *continuous evaluation program*. The key word here is continuous. The premises on which the hiring is done keep on changing depending upon the projects, processes, and changing policies. So, the safest way is to hire in bulk and then segregate the influx based on their performances and preferences. Again, there is a lot that depends upon many factors, and hence the acquisition process is handled by very talented people. The process of mass hiring is more suitable for the software industry than the core industries. The basic difference is the requirements are low in the management cadre in the core sectors. Maybe, we can compare the automobile sector with the software, but that also fades in comparison of numbers and salary. They employ more people on the lower side of the chain and they prefer people from polytechnics and simple graduates such as B.Sc. or B.Com. Moreover, there is a huge disparity in salaries. There is one more difference. The core industry does not maintain bench strength as compared to the software industry. The revenue models have something to do with this.

Before the world became global in recent centuries, and before all companies wanted to be leaders in the market, before they wanted to conquer the world and enjoy monopoly, before they started dealing in trillions, the world was simple. It was small. Each town had its team of skilled workers. They produced enough for their towns. They even customized their services. They delivered with involvement and love. The ruthlessness followed the unending greed. They destroyed the local talent, traditions, the individual needs and they controlled what is available. The famous sentence of Henry Ford when he launched his famous car Model "T," *"Any customer can have a car painted any color that he wants, so long as it is black."*, was perceived as a revolution. It may have but it was the start of some arrogance. The talents were replaced by the skills for the assembly of the cars, wherein a person repeated the same job for years to come. If he put wheels on the chassis, then he did for his entire life. *The assembly lines disassembled the earlier peaceful human lives.* The comfort of the industrial revolution came at a very high cost which we as humans are still contemplating. The earth, along with the sea, the space, was never so much disturbed as it is in the last five centuries. Before the industrial age, human greed was in control. Sadly, we cannot say so, now!

So, before any serious discussion on skill development, there has to be a detailed study of why we lost the skills. What worked so effectively for thousands of years was destroyed by human greed and the occupation of countries by overambitious and arrogant people. They were interested in the material resources. They looted the same and destroyed the culture and traditions of the occupied nations. The same trend is continued by companies like Amazon, Twitter, Facebook, and other virtual world giants. The world with things we could hold, feel, exchange, and produce, is on the slide. The misuse of the data and the ruthless race for control of the world without actually and physically occupying is more dangerous. The implications of data thefts, misuse, the ability to hold the world for ransom, and the complete financial world is at the mercy of companies that use the software. It takes a mad person at the top and the world order would be turned into chaos. The covid virus is a trailer as to what can be done by one small quantity of natural or artificial virus, (*Petri dish size*). It is said that the entire world was held at ransom for three years by just ten grams of the virus. Presently, there is news, making around that due to global warming the arctic glaciers are melting and they would release many hidden unforeseen viruses. It would be a terror if it is true.

It is possible to impart wisdom and skills can be inculcated and enhanced.

Once this simple fact is accepted the beginning can be made. The skills required can be identified, the sources can be focussed on, the training can be arranged, and the skills so imparted can be used for the betterment of society.

The mapping of the areas in a country for a specific skill can be a major step toward further belief-building measures. A weaver in Varanasi, or Yeola Maharashtra has to be sure that if he continues to weave the best sarees he would not die of hunger or frustration. The district-wise product identification is a great step and if it is not engulfed by the ever-present corruption and anti-nationals, it can be a game changer. Humans are smart. They understand the steps needed for making a great product but they are never sure of the help from the administration. And this has nothing to do with the developed, underdeveloped, developing, or countries named the third world, in all such types of worlds the farmers face the same problems, the industries face the same problems, the handicrafts are a diminishing trade, and so many new challenges are thrown by the inept handling by the *intelligent* people in the decision-making units.

The effort on a global scale is welcome for skill development. It has three basic areas. "This report is composed of three elements: the reasons why a skills strategy is needed; a conceptual framework for such a strategy; and recommendations for its effective implementation. These correspond to the three parts of the report, which address in turn the why, what, and how of equipping the workforce with the skills required for strong, sustainable, and balanced growth. Part I briefly describes selected drivers of longer-term change that challenge national skills development systems and provide the motivation for a commitment to improving them. Part II provides a conceptual framework for a skills development strategy, concerning national policy objectives, that is relevant to the diverse realities and needs of individual countries. Part III assembles the essential building blocks of a robust training strategy as called for by the G20 leaders, concerning a range of illustrations drawing on national examples" The 48 pages report published by the international labor organization is very promising and comprehensive and evokes hope. The details are on the link www.ilo.org/skills/WCMS_732185/lang--en/index.htm. And it is very interesting.

Any training for anything is very cost intensive, more so when it involves the training for the skills. The soft skills, along with the harder version of skills would in the future, are supposed to facilitate entry into the companies and later also sustain the person for his lifetime. If we are expecting so much from an activity spread over only some weeks then that activity needs to be comprehensively planned and executed. How many Institutes can pass the test? The pseudo activity in the name of placements is comparable to either a chicken moving after its head is chopped off or a bullock moving in circles extracting oil. Both of them move a lot but reach nowhere. There is movement and speed but without any direction. Most human beings these days are moving at a frantic speed but rarely reach anywhere they can be proud of. The students are no exceptions. The resources in terms of money, talent pool development, the actual training activity all over the world, and most importantly the successful implementation of the intended program are still a pipe dream. What is discussed in the initiation of any training program and what is said at the dissection of the same can very well summarise the point in contention. The extended and continuous effort on the part of all stakeholders is in question and generally, it is more for filling in the formats made mandatory by the regulating authorities who in themselves have participation minus the interest of the students. They formulate the rules regarding the sizes of the campuses, lecture halls, and labs. Also, the selection parameters of the teachers, professors, principals, **canteens, and even the toilet blocks**. They rarely speak about what a teacher should do once he enters the class or what he does. At least as of date, no mechanism can control the quality of teaching quality inside the classrooms. All controls concentrate on non-living aspects of the colleges. The question is simple: "If everything is so systematically *designed*, *planned,* and *executed* why the finished product is so bad?" Why engineers or managers are not up to the standards and norms of the industry? The reports from government agencies about the skills levels of the BEs, MBAs, and other graduates are very depressing and without any feasible solutions. There are a lot of words, tables, PowerPoint presentations, panel discussions, and many such pompous activities which are still in the discovery mode. What is achieved is not known, because the action taken reports are equally wordy and confusing. No person involved in these activities would be able to survive in the hardcore industry environment for long. One can read about such activity held and reported decades ago and the recent versions conducted now, and he would find very little difference. "*Why*", is the question never asked, if rarely asked by some impractical person it is never seriously taken and further answered logically. So, the situation continues! They say in management that if one does the same things for years the results would be the same. In the technical education sector, very qualified, wise, competent people are doing the **same things over the past few decades and are expecting different results.** The majority of teachers are not interested in participating in such activities involving placements but they are forced to participate. Attend any academic review meeting anywhere and you would know what is being discussed. How many charts are filled, how many papers are published in specified journals, how many conferences are attended, and how many are on the regulatory bodies, are the issues generally discussed by the people? The integrity issues of the teachers or the management are rarely addressed. Never a participant discusses the steps taken to teach properly, never mentioned that the students are better, due to the steps taken it is **proved that the performance** of the teachers is bad, because of the students. The low input quality, the language issues, the lack of discipline, the lack of infrastructure, the lack of quality laboratories, and many more such things are repeated over and over and again and again for decades and nothing is done about them. It is accepted because it suits the principal who also was a teacher before he became a principal and forgot teaching. (It is conveniently forgotten that some of the teachers are performing brilliantly in the same set of dreaded circumstances.) All such people are overly defensive and hence very aggressive when the reasons for the non-placeability of the students are discussed. They disassociate themselves from the activity as if it is something below dignity. Inside they know that they are the root cause of this inadequacy problem in the students. They could have taught in a better way, prepared the students for facing the corporate world more competently, could have been more involved, and helped the students to overcome the stigmas and the dogmas.

In such a scenario, the additional expense for the training is rarely granted. *What is the use*, they conveniently say, *you know the quality of our students*? This is accompanied by an *all-knowing* smile and the entire blame is shifted to the TPO. He carries the burden of the insufficient activity of the parents, the teachers, the administration, the principal, and the top management. Either he buckles or resigns and goes away. So, he is replaced by some other expendable pawn. Training and placement, as an activity, are never discussed except in the specific situation where some other college students are placed.

The developed world, the developing world, and the third world countries have problems in finding talent, and further developing the same. The inferences are strikingly similar. That talent is a *divine input* and it has nothing to do with the affluence of a family or a nation is still not understood properly. There are prejudices based on color, race, area, and the way of living, and everything is continued as it was in the pre-development era. People do not say but they follow the same old tracks believing seriously that their race is the best and deserves the best. They forget the history. They forget how their forefathers behaved with the rest of the world. There is very little acceptance of the fact that a person from a lesser-known place can be better and outclass the people of a better-known race. The presumptions and the assumptions are overpowering and the person from such a background has to prove that he is worthy to each one who matters and who does not. Also, it is not a one-time exercise, very often he is expected to repeat his test every time and for everyone. It is insulting, embarrassing, and often non-productive. The scenario is similar in the talent acquisition activity. Companies have their ways and means, procedures by which they seem to filter the candidates. The first filter is the towns and their tiering like ABC, metros and non-metros, institutions, and their ratings, they are so many that it becomes very confusing. Moreover, most companies forget that the responses both by the students and their institutes in the placements drive are customized and in the worst cases acquired. The reason for the future stresses is the difference between what is *presented* in the drive and what is *seen in actual work* conditions. The gap is wide and very rarely bridgeable.

What is not looked into in detail is all skill development programs talk about and conduct the improvement of specific skills. They very rarely concentrate or mostly forget the basic intelligence and skills of the person. When a person is absorbed and trained for a specific skill he can turn into a non-productive person shortly.

In the cases of Tata Administrative Services, Unilever, or Bajaj, selected people from the exclusive institutes and further spent a huge time, money, and training and converted a near-permanent resource. The attrition rate was manageable. The skill sets imbibed increase the security of the person and he tends to last in the company for a long period. Choose a good breed and then train it intensively, can rarely go wrong.

So, identifying potent skills of the interns, and honing, and training the skills for further use in the betterment of the individual and the organization is the main difference between these giants and the other companies. The dynamic and self-correcting system helps in the initial stages as well as in the long-term operations of the organizations.

Having talent is a gift of God, but in many cases, the usage is very poor. The ratio of people born with talent and the people who have successfully used the talent for the betterment of themselves and the organization is very low. The amount of money spent on training across the globe is a testimony to the gap between what is available and what is expected in professional lives.

Understanding management in a modern language is a process of dealing with and or controlling people, processes, and precedents, but in ancient Vedic philosophy, management begins with understanding oneself on the outer (Sthoolam) and the inner side (Sooksham) in such a thorough fashion that we can use the same in the betterment of the world we live in. Knowing something, and mastering something are two different things and the trainer must be able to stress the need of mastering at least one skill that would bring in his livelihood and some secondary skill that would bring relief in his life. The secondary skill should be learned in such a way that if needed the same can be potent enough to earn a livelihood. Some skills are universally accepted and others are more localized. Both are important and can produce excellent results. Understanding the resource in its entirety is complex, but once done you can create something great. Like if we understand gold or copper or iron in a way, we should then we can create so many different things and better our world. The trainer also has to understand the trainee in such a minute way that he can create a person who can deliver and that too on a long-term scale.

Skills are a dynamic phenomenon.

We are aware that different times demand different levels of skills, and different sectors need different skills. Similarly, different companies need different skills. The only common factor in all these combinations is human beings. Thankfully there is a huge sample of human beings to select from. The skill complements in humans are infinite, and if we try to categorize it is almost impossible. So, the organizations try to channel their sample of skill sets and then try to match the candidates with their requirements. It is not at all easy as it is not once done and the rest is a fine job, but the same human has to adapt to the changing and dynamic needs of the organization. There is nothing like a perfect match and even if it happens once in a while, it would rarely continue to be so over some time. Out of the skills, the most hyped in the past few decades are referred to as soft skills. When the concept was launched it was as if they had found the ultimate answers to all problems. There were seminars, training, and a new boom season for the English-speaking people, they were helped by the psychologists and yet today we find that nothing much has changed concerning the skill sets of the placements aspiring students. It is a fact that most students in engineering, management, and other streams cannot express themselves in any language leaving aside English. An understanding of soft skills is a must for all trainers and planners of skills.

The sudden and urgent need for soft skills is a clear indication that conventional business methods and tactics are seen as not enough for the sustained growth of any business. The business may grow but the desirable continuous sustenance, along with the required parameters, does need specific efforts. The efforts can be a normal 9 to 5, which may be out of compulsion or very rarely out of the self-will and belief that whatever is done would be for the ultimate good of the organization and the common public at large.

The problem with soft skills is very peculiar. It may not be in the form of a short-term, easy-to-do, **'once done last forever'** pattern. On the contrary, it is seen as a culmination of various seemingly insignificant, outwardly unrelated, at times even boring activities. The judgment regarding whether you have soft skills comes not from you but from the people you deal with and hence it becomes that much more difficult. One set of responses, which is accepted as correct by one group of customers may not be accepted by the other, so one starts thinking about what is that each individual wants as a soft skill.

Is there any set pattern, which may pass the law of percentages?

Can we develop a module, which would guarantee at least a minimum level of performance, as far as the products and services side is concerned? The answer is again yes and no.

As a policy decision-maker, one has to understand that the rules laid down by themselves are not usually sufficient to deliver the desired results, but the major contribution comes from the way the rules are practiced in actual on-the-job situations by every stakeholder. In an attempt to find the gospel truths regarding soft skills, people tend to deal with the wrong cards and create self-created confusion. Further, how it is practiced assumes tremendous importance in the process of being either accepted by the customers or summarily rejected and ridiculed as an organization with no ability. The image creation of the organization should be the objective of such training activity and hence soft skills ability forms the backbone of the image-building process.

Before launching into a soft skills activity, one has to understand some basic things, such as:

1. That it is **not a replacement** for a lack of knowledge,
2. That it is a **valuable addition to the core** exercise,
3. That it needs a continuous and most importantly **voluntary** effort from the one who wishes to practice it,
4. That it needs **constant up-gradation.**

Most of the time when a person is not able to speak in the way he should, the *main reason* cited is the lack of soft skills. It is very convenient and suits everyone. The fact that the person may be an original dumbo or that he may not have *anything to speak* is forgotten. The question of soft skills or their absence comes as the second most important thing; the first is obviously knowledge! The message forms an important part of the communication process and to create a correct message one has to start working on what he wants to say.

Is his information correct?

Is it properly authenticated?

Is it of any interest to the audience?

What is the novelty angle?

The person should ask himself that if he has to swap his place with the audience would he be interested in the matter he is supposed to present?

If **the message is right,** then and then only, the question of soft skills arises. Even a polished talker finds it extremely difficult to talk when he has nothing interesting to say.

Lots have been said about the verbal and nonverbal variety of communication, so much so that everyone feels that he knows about these things. The problem is that most such people have no or at best rudimentary ideas, further the problem is even if he knows what he does about the same. The fact is that even today we have a big percentage of the **Hari Sadu** (the obnoxious boss in the advertisement) in the industry and the so-called corporate world. Further, the worst part is that these people are responsible for the evaluations and the dreaded appraisals. Soft skills **do not** and I repeat **do not come** automatically because you are a boss. Whoever, you may be, you still have to acquire the soft skills and more importantly practice them before you expect them to exist in your staff. Sadly, the picture is exactly reversed and the situation is grim. Let us acknowledge that soft skills as well as their training are an expert's job.

The theory of soft skills is at a rudimentary stage, and the practice of corporate soft skills is in the neo-natal stage. Even today a person with a *pack of butter* is preferred to a committed version which spells the basic reason for the failure in the system.

The commonly required soft skills are as follows:

1. Communication skills
2. Computer skills
3. Self-management skills
4. Social etiquette
5. Interpersonal skills
6. Teamwork skills
7. Leadership skills
8. Learning skills
9. Presentation skills

Basic skills remain the same. Monster.com people have identified some twenty-six skills as classified soft skills- it is pretty exhaustive! It is indicative and it helps to design the training needs.

1. Oral communication skills
2. Written communication skills
3. Honesty
4. Teamwork/ Collaboration skills
5. Self-Collaboration skills/ initiative
6. Work ethics/ dependability
7. Critical thinking
8. Risk-taking ability
9. Flexibility/adaptability
10. Organization skills
11. Leadership skills
12. Interpersonal skills

13. Working under pressure/stress management
14. Questioning skills
15. Creativity
16. Influencing skills
17. Research skills
18. Organization skills
19. Problem-solving skills
20. Multicultural skills
21. Computer skills
22. Learning skills
23. Detail orientation
24. Quantitative skills
25. Teaching/ training skills
26. Time management skills

In ancient India, we had 64 skills (*Kala*) identified for a student. In the famous finishing schools in Switzerland, they teach a girl to be a lady in the upper crest of society. They teach social etiquette, table manners, and polite conversation while mingling in society functions, something like Rose in the famous Titanic movie.

The point to be understood here is simple. The TPO has to rationalize the input of the training content. He has to restrict the soft skills training limited to get a placement. If the student is so willing, he can learn all skills needed for his advancement in his chosen career. If the delivery mix is bungled the student would be overloaded and at the end of the training sessions he would be as disinterested, disillusioned, and confused as he was before the skills training.

I always feel that the students **were taught all essential soft skills** in any normal Indian family by their parents. Students before their teenage are usually well-behaved. They eat, talk, greet, knock on the door before they enter a room, walk softly, and answer diligently but after a while, they forget every good thing and literally turn into brats. At a later stage, they have to be taught all normal manners, etiquette, and communication of various types in a very painful and tedious way. A very long time is wasted in achieving the zero level and making the students teachable.

Moreover, with the speed, at which talent acquisition takes place in the present corporate hiring, one can be happy if he knows what he wants and to what extent he can be satisfied. Mass hiring combined with mass training and mass induction is almost impersonal and most of the stakeholders tend to forget that they are dealing with individual and living human beings. No HR person would ever agree, at least in public, to this. They would try to convince you with their impeccably designed training programs, and they would throw a lot of statistics on your face to prove their point, but inside their honest minds, they know that they are a part of a whirlwind with no end in the sight. If their process is so complete and comprehensive their insecurity is very hard to explain. Very few modern HRs can be compared to the old-timers in the personnel departments. The learning and development department in most companies talks about great things without realizing that they are putting their foot in the mouth. They have yet to prove any direct linkage between what they do under the name of development with the extended and continuous productivity of a person. They talk in a language that is full of preconditions and assumptions. **Only human beings need artificial training in life skills**. So, unless he wants to be, he cannot be trained. But at the same time, we have to concede that they are flowing against the current.

We have to accept that the training and the other departments like Learning and development are trying their best with limited resources, as no company is ready to accept that profit is secondary to human development. Maybe we are trying to find the right mix and the right path to the right combination of training, learning, and profits.

***

CHAPTER XIII

Jobs in the Future

Jobs in the Future

There are two sides to any coin, we knew since we were in school.

Jobs is one such term. It is an indicator of the development in a nation, and prosperity of the nation. This one aspect of commerce keeps on changing very fast and very silently. By the way, when the policymakers become aware, the scales of the issue go out of hand. So, it is better to have some idea about the comparison between the jobs in the present day and the jobs of the future.

Jobs of the future is an interesting subject, and the other side of it is *the future of jobs*. As it is in the last two decades the nature of the jobs, the selection procedures, and the designations of the hiring side have just plainly changed. It would have been very hard for somebody in the nineteen seventies to just imagine that a single company would employ thousands of people at a single time and that too year after year. The salaries offered, the prospects of working overseas, the phenomenal stock options, and the new terms like a team, team leaders, and projects manager, were unheard of. But today they are as common as sand on a beach.

The latest to hit the job market is the concept of WFH, work from home. Due to really unforeseen circumstances, allegedly manmade, which created the pandemic situation in the world. The covid 19, hit all of us in a way nothing before in the last few centuries. The worst hit was the almost arrogant planning of the corporate giants. The WFH is so spectacularly horrible that many books would be written on it in the coming years.

For us, WFH is one of the perspectives which changed the future of the jobs, the selection processes, the on-board process, the induction training of the freshly hired employees, the control, the supervision, and even the appraisals. One of the HR people even predicted the end of the offices, lush premises, canteens, and posh training centres, like Infosys, TCS, and other giants. What part of the present processes would be retained and what else would be discarded is a topic of intense discussion. The review and the conclusions thereafter would affect the way people would be hired, the skills for which they would be hired, further trained, and appraised in the coming few years.

The intense impact of the virtual world, the almost absence of daily commutation to the workplace and back home, the ease with which the multinational controls are accomplished, the more and more digitization, huge savings on the expenses like rent, power bills, license fees of the software's is too big to ignore.

The lifestyles of the people in Pune, Bangalore, Chennai, Mumbai, Gurgaon, California, New Jersey, and many other places in the world have been altered due to WFH. One small whim of nature has taught us that we as a human race have a lot to learn. The comfort of the known and the optimistic planning collapsed like a proverbial castle of playing cards. We have started to rebuild and while we are at it many new things are automatically included in the processes. We are wary and weighing the impacts. It has been accepted as the change which is staying with us for some time to come.

One effect of the endemic was that there is a boom in the pharma, surgical, and services sectors of the industry. People made huge money when the world was actually on the verge of a standstill. There would be new ways of making money. The new ways would need new talents. The time taken for the entire exercise of need identification to the product design and subsequent supply would be less. It would mean smarter and faster people, who would work overtime and enjoy the incentives more than the salary. If we have to use the language of HR, we would say that the HR departments would look for a lean and thin agile organization with real-time business models. The department would need to be very alert to the changing needs of the environment. They would work very proactively and would constantly juggle between the permanent on-roll employees along with contractual, consultant, outsourced, and freelancers.

The future organizations would be smooth and at the same time very ruthless. The result-oriented approach is very good to talk about but it spells doom for the slow employees. Slow as in the case of those who do not change as per the needs of the organization. Earlier the organizations took a longer time to identify the slow movers, now they can identify and do away with laggers very fast. The students have to understand that mere getting into a posh organization is not enough they would have to be on their toes to get retained rather than retrenched. At the end of each day month or quarter, HR would be appraising and taking some unpleasant decisions.

Good people are scarce.

What makes your students good is a dynamic phenomenon. Because they have to remain good in the future too. The parameters change every year. What the minor and major deviations would be from the last year, are to be identified by the TPO, or else he would end up in the also-ran category. The ratio between the number of jobs available and the number of applicants has changed. Less number of able people are in the line as compared to the earlier times in the case of specific talents. The job descriptions have become more elaborate. The job profiles are more customized and very specific. The trend of training the incoming candidates is also as per the actual application in the company. HR and talent acquisition people are not interested in taking people and then training them later, but they would be making the needs very specific and clear so that the training activity is minimal and the productivity is optimized.

On the other side where we have the core functions industry, the continuous process industries, the power companies, the hospitals, the transports like railways or international travel have faced altogether different sets of problems. Core industries are more stable as compared to the software version. Their requirements are less in number. Once employed the candidate would be in a better frame of mind as he would be in a groove and would have time to learn and adapt.

The service industry was affected the worst, but they somehow managed to stay afloat despite very testing time in the endemic. People from the service industry deserve a special pat on the back for what they did during the covid 19 time. There is a boom in the service sector, but it is for the lower levels of jobs rather than the executive cadre. Their working model is mostly bottom heavy. They do not need very highly qualified people in the operations. Most of the operations are AI controlled. They are a type of faceless organization where human interfaces are low, and yet at the contact point, they would need a huge number of qualified people mostly from ITI instead of IITs.

Automation and its effects. Ever since the first machine was designed and commissioned the debate started about how it would affect human workers. The classic debate continues, but the aspects and perspectives are constantly changing. The use of machines and web technology is so high these days that we are practically surrounded by machines and AI for all our routine and advanced activities. It is estimated that about seventy-five percent of the total GDP is driven by machines in countries like UK or Sweden.

Earlier the performance of the machine largely depended upon the operators using them. Now machines are getting smarter as we term them so in a way, they reshape the demands of the persons who use them. Most of the training is about upgrading the workforce to be able to use the newer generations of machines. Machines for medical treatments can be a good example. The onset of AI has made machines analytical about their performances and even they can self-correct their operations. The aspects of quality, flexibility in the operations, optimizing yields, reducing consumption of energy, conforming to national and international standards, and many such inputs would be controlled by machines. One person in the control room is the main characteristic of future operations. Like what has happened in ticketing, insurance, banking, as well as treasuries and revenue departments. The initial settings would be done by the human components and the rest would be handled by the machines.

The students both in engineering as well as MBA have to understand the following points to be able to enter and survive in the professional organization they join. Let us understand one by one.

1. **Change your thinking**. The operating managers have to adapt from controlling the human workforce to the control of machines. Humans are naturally flexible and hence adapt faster to minor changes in the operating environment. He can adjust a valve and set the pressures right. But when controlled by a machine it becomes a complex issue. The machine does not understand any logic other than what it is programmed for. So, these days a term called think lean is popular. The machines can work faster, with more accuracy but they need more specific instructions in their language. So, the students need to learn to communicate with machines in the specific language the machines understand.
2. **Inflexibility**: We know that humans are flexible and they learn as they walk along the process. They discard the old and adapt to the new. The machines are incapable of this and hence they are inflexible. In a way it is good but in the other case, it hurts. So, the performance of a machine in various conditions cannot be automatic. It has to be conditioned and calibrated. The managers have to think like a machine and instructions have to be extremely specific.
3. **Variability**: The variables whether in the raw materials, designs, or processes affect the overall productivity. Hence lean organizations

would aim at fixing the procedures in such a way that the consistency in quality of the raw material, and the processes. It is not simple but these days managers have learned to maintain a certain control and achieve consistent delivery of desired results over a long period.

4. **Controlling the waste**: The wastage in various forms such as raw materials, and overproduction, needs to be kept under control so that the customer is served properly.
5. **In many companies** a trend is followed in which they treat employees as internal customers, so they are segmented just like the consumers in the market.
6. **Focus on** the organization's culture and acceptance of diversity. Very few employees realize the culture of their companies unless they quit and join other companies. The new joining talent is supposed to learn and maintain the culture as well as the basic decorum. As regards diversity it is now accepted that a company with diverse groups would perform better than closed cultures. **Diversity is treated as an asset**. The diversity in age, gender, even sexual orientation, background, language, ethnicity, and many such parameters is treasured and maintained.
7. **Goal-oriented** approach: The MBO is again stressed in the daily working of the organization. The goals, objectives, and outcomes are all different names but they all can be achieved only when the people in the organization identify themselves with the same. Goals are only understood and worked upon by human beings. The matching of the assignment with the correct employee is the magic done by very few organizations and it is a dynamic and continuously changing matrix. The students have to understand and somehow fit into the groove.
8. **Avoiding myopia**: One of the most harmful conditions is when the organization believes in the myth of continuing with success. Whatever they have been doing, they would keep doing and they would get the same results. **It does not work that way**. There are many examples in India, and international companies. You may just search on google and be informed. Companies have been washed down due to the rigidity both in products and in personnel.
9. **Concept of profit**: In the earlier days people refrained from talking about profit. It was almost a bad word. These days however organizations do talk about profits and profitability. The recent concept is that the profit is calculated on an hourly basis. What a man or a machine should do to achieve the profit goals is a new parameter. When the performance

of a machine was calculated on a daily, weekly, or monthly basis, things were less dynamic. Now with the market being global and geographical distribution almost impossible, one has to monitor the performance on an hourly base. One degree deviation can mean a loss or gain of billions.

One of the most vital and dynamic issues that a TPO has to effectively tackle is the fact that every few years the nature of the job changes. He has to work on a time scale of 18 to 24 months and keep it rolling with accurate data and its analysis. If he can create even a rough simulation scenario his students would be more aware of the new techniques prevalent at that time in the companies. Each sector would have a different set of parameters about which the TPO must be aware. The jobs, their selections, their training, and their salaries TPO has to be aware of. He has to find a way to apply his information to the best possible effect and get his students placed.

***

CHAPTER XIV

The Actual Process

The Actual Process

The actual process of campus placement is relatively simple. If everyone in the process was involved the students would be different. They would be confident, clear, and correct in their approach toward the placement. They would know what they want and more importantly how to get the same.

One of the foremost things the students have to remember is that the placement drive is a **POSITIVE** Process. The company people want the maximum number of students to get selected. Anyone telling the students anything else should not be trusted by the students. A lot of people would talk about a lot of unwanted and unfair things, but then that is a part of our civilized society. We cannot change the same, so the students should concentrate on the success stories in their colleges and hope that their campus drive is fair. The advice of being positive really helps here.

The issue is if nobody wishes to put in the required effort in the process the result would not match the expectations. In an MBA course, the first three semesters are done without a thought to the Placements. Whereas in the engineering course the first six semesters are *devoted* to academics. Sadly, in both cases, the students do not appear prepared for the Placement process. The teachers simply disown the students. The raw, untreated, presumptuous sample of students falls in the laps of even more unprepared TPO. The multiplication of unwilling zeros results in an even bigger zero. The TPO has to realize what a willing zero can achieve if it is placed properly in a number.

STEPWISE CAMPUS PLACEMENT DRIVE

Weightage/ 100 %

Step 1. CV /Resume 5%

Step 2. Aptitude Tests 35%

Step 3. Group Discussion 30%

Step 4. Personal Interview 25 %

Step 5. HR Personal Interview 5%

The percentages displayed are again representative and in actual conditions, they may be mixed in a different way. For example, in an engineering campus drive, the GD is generally not done. (Except in cases, where the placements are intended for a job in marketing or PR.) So, in such cases, the AT gets the weightage of 65% instead of 35%.

The above chart is a representative depiction of the process. Various companies have their own variations but they are rare and far between. The variations may include psychological testing, J2M (J2M is just two minutes. It is an instant and ex tempore exercise where the candidate picks up a topic chit from a bowl and speaks for two minutes. It is not at all easy and needs a lot of practice), or a JAM session (It is just a minute and is similar to J2M except for the time). Psychological testing is very effectively used in the selection of the army and other services. The TAT /PAT tests, (Thematic Appreciation Test and Picture Appreciation Test) are great but not very frequently used in the campus recruitment drives hence we do not discuss them here. PAT can also be a psychological aptitude test but again not very often used in campus drives.

What is suggested, however, is that the students should appear for an SSB interview before they go for campus drives. SSB interviews are very intensive and cover a lot of things very relevant for clearing the GD and PI. SSB interviews are conducted with a lot of empathy and can be a real positive factor. And if the candidate clears the SSB he is assured of dignified life in the defence forces. Students in our institute were greatly helped by the SSB experience. Navy, Air Force, and military regularly conduct drives for SSB sometime around August/ September.

What is to be understood by the TPO and his students is that the drive process is somewhat like a **treasure hunt**. One cannot proceed to the next round unless he clears the earlier round. At the same time, each round has its significant contribution to the ultimate selection of the candidate.

Let us once again understand each step:

1. **CV/Resume/ Bio-data**: The Curriculum Vitae literally means the course of life for a person. It is an organized presentation of the personal details, education, skills, work experience, accomplishments, references, and any other such thing which would facilitate the selection of the candidate. The CV should be restricted to two pages and exceptional cases three pages. It is a thumb rule, nothing more.

Resume: It literally means summary in French. So, one should try to summarise the personal details along with the most relevant details of the skill set, experience, and accomplishments. A resume may not include all details of the profile. The limit should be ideally one page.

Bio-data: Bio-Data is a shorter version of the term biographical data. It is an old-time word and now we rarely use this. It gives details of a person in a chronological fashion and in details. There is no limit on pages.

The most important thing about a CV that is to be understood by all concerned is the simple fact that the **contents matter more** than the style of presentation. Also, a **stylish CV template cannot add value to a mediocre candidate**. It is seriously felt that the CV aspect is unnecessarily hyped in the placement process. What you have done during your college tenure, plus what extra, apart from your usual academics, you have achieved, during the same period would **add value to the CV**. Value additions like certifications, a diploma in a foreign language, volunteering, participation in international seminars, and articles published, are what the students must aim for rather than the style of template. **As it is the college would have its own prescribed format of the resume so all information about all students would look more or less the same.** Ordinary trainers find this topic the easiest so they keep on talking about the same.

There are more than thousands of different templates making rounds in various colors, shapes, and styles but without worthwhile content, they are all as tasteless as food without salt. In a campus drive, when the students of the same institute are being evaluated the importance of a CV is limited to the basic information of the candidate. Moreover, most colleges have a standard format for the CV.

- One thing which should be always ensured is that all relevant and important details are on the right-hand side of the CV.
- All educational details should be in a tabular form and not in the text.
- Accomplishments must be highlighted.
- Project details need to be highlighted.
- All other things such as hobbies, and family details, can be mentioned if the space allows.
- Ladies should share contact numbers only if their TPO allows them to.

So, a CV/resume/ bio-data would be required to present all your relevant details in an acceptable format. **One line rule** is to write only that which you can substantiate and discuss. CV is the basis on which your interview would be handled by the interviewer. Do not write, because somebody else has written, it is a certain trap for failure.

1. **Aptitude Test**: The second step in the actual process is the major filter to weed out undesirable candidates. Most students treat AT very casually. Their teachers are party to the same. This is confirmed by the data provided by AICTE and other agencies. The data says that only 15 to 20 percent of students clear the AT. So plainly speaking out of one hundred aspirants 85 to 80 students are eliminated from the further process.

- Mind you the tests are not very tough.
- Their patterns are declared well in advance.
- The students know what to expect but they do not perform.
- The percentages of the students clearing the AT decrease even further if the negative marking is in force.
- The data is in force for quite a few decades but the trend is not changing.
- The percentages are not improving in any appreciable way.

The only reason is that the students do not practice enough. They believe that they would clear the AT because they think they are intelligent. It does not work out that way. The problem lies in the number of questions, time allotted, negative marking, wrong approach, and most importantly lack of practice. The papers are so designed that the student cannot complete the mere reading of the question paper, leaving aside solving the problems.

The only way to be confident about **clearing the AT is to be able to take 60 tests/ exams in a week with a score above 85**. Your mind has to be tuned to such a level that you should sense the answer when you read the question. You put that value and recheck the answer. You would save a lot of time, otherwise, you would be almost attempting 400 questions instead of 100.

It is suggested that complete seriousness is absolutely essential to clear the AT. If you do not clear the AT, **all your marks, or grades are insufficient** to get a good placement. There are many books for each aspect of AT. One minute search on the net would give you hundreds of them. If you cannot clear the AT, you are losing about five to six lakhs rupees in the first year of your career. And in the next twenty years, the amount can be in millions. **What further motivation, the student needs is beyond the common logic.** One simple test is all that one has to clear.

We are providing a detailed essay that should give any willing student an initiation into the matter of AT.

Aptitude Tests.

Ever since mankind has opted for the division of labor, the problem of finding the right man for the right job has been noticed. After thousands of years, even today, the problem still persists. There has been a lot of methodical research, which has included different sampling procedures, spread over dozens of nations, human races, sex ratios, genetic data, details about the races, and skills passed over from generation to generation, and yet we cannot for sure say that we can find a right man for a right job. To my mind this is more due to the immense diversity mankind possesses rather than the efficacy of the testing procedures. Even if the tests give the right man initially, there is very little guarantee that the right man would continue to be right in the years to come. The issue is vastly complicated and finding an answer depending on a single dimension is a little bit tricky. As the entire process involves the man, both as a candidate and as an evaluator, a lot of subjectivity creeps in. With subjectivity, many other angles such as presumptions, prejudices, and pressures from various sources, certain compulsions automatically walk in. And yet man has not rightly given up the hope of finding an objective way of selecting the right man for the right job. In the early years of the last century, Aptitude Tests have been extensively used to monitor the process of selecting a suitable person for a job in question. It has been documented that the tests are nearest to the most objective way we can get to. The testing is very interesting and I try to give you an insight into the same.

Before we go any further let us first understand "Aptitude." The dictionary (Collins Cobuild) describes aptitude ***as an ability to learn a particular thing easily and quicklyand to do it well***. Further, it also describes the aptitude test ***as a test specially designed tofind out how easy and how well you can do something***.

Webster's new dictionary and the thesaurus describe aptitude as Ability, aptness, bent, capability, capacity, cleverness, disposition, flair, inclination, knack, penchant, talent, and many such words.

Again, when we talk of aptitude tests, we should have a predefined set of qualities we are looking for in the prospective candidate. More importantly, we should not subsequently fall for any pressures to change the same. Otherwise, we are definitely heading for a huge waste of time, energy, and money. It is observed that there is a marked tendency to **lowerthe bar** to accommodate second class, (as there is a dearth of first-class people) and selections are made. This results in further complications and the second class very rarely fulfills the requirement of the job. Hence, conducting the aptitude tests and their subsequent evaluation needs a special person.

In the recent past, the tests were not as much needed as they are today. The reason seems to be the gradual delinking of the learning aspect with the education degrees, dished out to the undeserving. Hence, it becomes even more important to find out a way that can possibly give us a decent enough approach to find suitable candidates for a job or for a curriculum. The aptitude tests may serve this purpose if (and only if) conducted in the right spirit and manner.

Types of aptitude tests:

The main types of tests are as follows:

1. Psychological tests
2. Group tests
3. Situational tests

1. **Psychological Tests.**

These tests are designed in such a way that the **psyche** of the prospective candidate is often put to test in a controlled fashion and the responses are monitored against the normal sample. Various types of tests are as below:

a. Intelligence tests
b. Projective personality tests.
a. Intelligence tests: They mainly have

i. Verbal tests
ii. Non-verbal tests

b. Projective personality tests.

i. Word association tests
ii. Thematic appreciation tests
iii. Psychological Situational tests.

The intelligence test is a collection of problems arranged in ascending order of difficulty, which a candidate is required to solve within a specified time limit. The underlying principle is that a more intelligent person would be able to attempt and solve more problems than a lesser intelligent person. The problems may be in the form of sums, pictures, letters, patterns, or any other similar material available at the site of the test, which would decide whether or not a person could relate, perceive, and appreciate the relationship between the different objects within a specified time limit.

The projective Personality tests are conducted to induce a response to a given stimulus from the candidate. The stimuli again are in the form of words, pictures, or situations. The examiner who is generally a trained psychologist then evaluates the candidate for his personality traits.

The projective personality tests are conducted to check out the common traits, which are as follows:

a. The basic desires,
b. Mental conflicts,
c. Attitude towards others,
d. Handling the stress,
e. Power of reasoning,
f. Their determination to succeed and even his social attributes
g. Usually, the examiner tries to generate a pen picture of the candidate. The marks are awarded accordingly.

2. **The Group Tests.**

The group tests as the name suggest involve the groups and the candidate's performance in a group. The candidates are supposed to perform many tasks either collectively or individually, but always in the association of a group. Some of the more known forms are group discussions, group planning, case studies, and solutions to given situations, leadership exercises. The more recent addition is situational testing in actual or practical conditions. What has been found on the basis of the experiences in the industry is that the behavior of the candidate in the group is far more important than his individual capacity. Ultimately, he has to perform in the group and for the group. The response of the candidate is measured on the following criteria.

i. His influence on the group
ii. The influence of the group on him
iii. Whether or not he can identify himself with the group
iv. His commitment to the interests of the group
v. His ability to cooperate

vi. His ability to accept criticism
vii. Whether he is accepted by the group or not.

The examiner should also look for the

i. Drive
ii. Enthusiasm
iii. Power of expression
iv. Consistency
v. Leadership qualities
vi. Power of reasoning and convincing the others in the group
vii. Risk-taking ability
viii. And even the temper.

There are different versions of tests for checking the aptitude of candidates.

1 **Word Association Tests (WAT)**: One has to write a sentence on a given word. Say, plane/ wire/pc/ girl/ teacher/ pen/ and any other common word.

2 **Thematic Appreciation Test (TAT):** various slides are shown, and one has to write the story or what he thinks about the same. 30 to 45 seconds are for viewing and 3 minutes are for writing. The tricky slides are the black slides, blank slides, or with abstract backgrounds. Here the candidate has to imagine and write something really original

3 **Psychological Situation Tests:** About 30 questions are asked based on the various common day-to-day situations. They also call it -what **Theo** or **X** would do in a given situation.

4 **Self-story leading to self-appraisal:** If one is not able to talk about him, it should be a matter of serious concern. That is not as easy as everyone thinks but probably is the most difficult assignment. One has to manage to highlight all his plus points without appearing arrogant, or even overbearing. The following four would be some serious pointers for writing an effective self-story.

a. Why he thinks is suitable for the said job?
b. What he wants to be in the near future?
c. What are his plans for this?
d. Positive impacts in his life

The tests take a very steep road when they are conducted for premier institutes or national admissions. To discuss in brief and just to give an idea let us talk about the CAT for top-class management institutes and the GMAT for studies abroad as well as the IITs.

The basic structure of the tests is given below. It may change from time to time.

CAT (Common Admission Test) has three sections:

1) Language Section: It consists of passages followed by questions based on them and objective questions such as pick the odd word out of the given four; which is the correct antonym/synonym out of the four words or pick out the word with the wrong spelling or correct spelling from the four given options etc. All questions are M.C.Q.s (Multiple Choice Questions)

2) Arithmetic Section (mathematics.) The questions are based on Time, Speed and Distance; Ratio and Proportion; Probability; Trigonometry; Geometry. All questions are MCQs.

3) Logical Section: Here you have two sections:

a. Logical Reasoning: Questions like if A is the father of B but B is not the son of A, then what is the relationship between A and B?
b. Data Interpretation: Here you are given pie diagrams or bar charts or any form of statistical diagram and you are asked relevant questions.

GMAT

The Graduate Management Admission Test (GMAT) consists of three parts.

1) **Verbal Section**: Three types of MCQs are used in the Verbal section of the GMAT Exam—

Reading Comprehension,
Critical Reasoning, and
Sentence Correction.

2) **Quantitative Section:** Two types of MCQs are used in the Quantitative section

Problem Solving and
Data Sufficiency.

Both types of questions require knowledge of:

Arithmetic,
Elementary algebra, and

Commonly known concepts of geometry.

3) **Analytical written Assessment Section:** It is designed as a direct measure of your ability to think critically and to communicate your ideas. The AWA consists of two 30-minute writing tasks—

Analysis of an Issue

and

Analysis of an Argument.

The issues and arguments presented in the test relate to topics of general interest, business, or a variety of other subjects. Specific knowledge of the essay topic is not necessary; only your capacity to write analytically is assessed.

The above two are the tests of intelligence at a sustained level. The degree of difficulty is as it is very high and gets further tough because of the smaller number of seats versus the huge number of applicants. If you have any doubts you should try to attempt the sample tests. If you feel you have very good English try to solve the questions in the comprehension passages in the SBI PO Tests. You are likely to find that they are very tough. India is a lucky nation where there is no dearth of expert advice. And we all implore you all to avail the same from the correct variety of experts.

Testing of the aptitudes in Practical Situations.

Most managers develop their own methods for testing the candidates fitting for their own fields. There is very little to describe or justify the means but they tend to find an acceptable level of candidates. The common examples can be:

- Candidates are made to wait for hours,
- Even if the interviews are canceled,
- Somebody gives them serious hiding without any apparent reason,
- They are told to perform some menial tasks,
- Unnecessary abuse of their Institute or their previous employer.

I remember one incident where six candidates were waiting for an interview for an office boy.

The room they were made to the seat was very bad, untidy, and filthy. The candidate who cleaned the room was selected without a single question. The others were not suitable.

Why present days these tests are not producing the results expected of them is a relatively simple question. The mushroomed institutes of CAT/

MAT/ NET/ GATE/ GMAT coach their students day in and day out. I do not have anything against but then the **purpose** of these tests was to find out **natural** aptitude and not **practiced or conditionedaptitude.** The results in such cases would be most absurd.

The formats of all types of tests are available in the books, including the psychological ones. It is very tempting for many organizations to utilize them. What is to be clearly understood is the fact that it is not the test, but the subsequent analysis of the candidates by the competent authorities is the key to meeting the standards. What a psychologist can decipher from the test is quite different than what a layman can do.

The basic thing needed to have an effective aptitude test is that the persons who conduct it should believe in it and that they do not fall prey to shortcuts. If the complete procedure is followed it is more likely to produce better results. Finding a person with a correct in-built aptitude is the objective of the aptitude tests, which is very vital in the future part of the career path of the person. Whether he becomes a technocrat or a general manager he is required to operate on at least two distinct levels. The first is of the normal routine operations and the second is when the system is under a stress. The person with the inbuilt aptitude is more likely to succeed in the stressed stage, where one wrong decision has a cascading and long-term damaging effect. So, aptitude tests assume a great deal of significance.

Intelligence tests:

1

Analogy test:

As good is to As good is to bad happiness is to -------- sorrow

As food is to eating the newspaper is to------- reading.

2

Sentence formation

Rearrange the sentences so as to make them meaningful. Help god those who help ---------themselves

3

General Knowledge test

Ranchi is the capital of Jharkhand yes/no

The highest rainfall in the world is at Cherapunji. Yes/no

4

Verbal relation

Mayor city/ captain

Store, ship, library general ship

5

Common sense questions

A is the father of B, but B is not the son of A. what is the relationship of A and B? Daughter

6

Completion test

Make a new word by adding one letter (not S) to the following.

Pain *t* /Hop *e*/ Unit *y*/ Arm *y*/ Tas *k*/ Sk *y*/

7

Series test

What is the next in the series?

10,5,9,5,8,5..........---------*7*

6,7,5,8,4,9,...........---------*5*

8

Jumbled words

Rearrange the letters to form a word.

EBAR *BEAR* OTLSU *LOTUS*

9

Synonym test

Pick up the correct word from the bracket, which corresponds to the one outside the bracket.

Disloyal (faithful, unfair, sinner, *treacherous)*

Extravagant (Careful, spendthrift, careless, miser, *lavish)*

10

One Word Substitution

Fill in the blank space with the correct word.

He does not believe in God *Atheist*

He collects stamps *Philatelist*

11

Word Fitting

Write words that begin and end with the same letter

Or write words that begin with say *t* and end with *l trail*

12

Letter difference

There are groups of letters given below. Find the odd one.

ABCF GHIL MNOR *RSTW* DCBA HGFE MRVX PONM

13

Alphabetical tests

Answer the following on the basis of alphabet.

ABCD EFGH IJKLM NOPQ RSTU VWXYZ

-Write down the *seventh* letter after *q*.

-*Ninth* letter from the letter *l* in the reverse.

14

Coding and Decoding

The words below are the codes; write the *italic words* in code

Reach= tgcej Nagpur= lyensp

Early quite general

15

Multiple Choice tests

Pick up the correct choice out of four or five

It is generally safe to judge the character of a man by

a. his outward appearance

b. his wealth

c his associates

d *his actions*

e his wife

16

Absurdity.

You have to identify the absurdity in the statements.

The boys were very angry. They threw stones at each other. All stones were round and very light. They floated in the air before landing.

17

Direction tests

You travel towards the south 5.5 km, then turn to the east and walk 3kms. Then turn left and walk 2kms. How far you are from the starting point?

18

Spot the stranger

One word in the group that is different.

RED/ BLUE/ WHITE/ *COTTON* /GREEN

19

Sums

Ages, distances, water filling/leakages, etc

The best friends of the students are people like R.S. Agrawal, Shakuntala Devi, and a few other authors who have written books on lateral thinking.

Also, there are many tests on the net which give you an idea of what to expect and how to approach it.

3. <u>GD</u>: <u>GROUP DISCUSSION</u>: The next mass scale filter is in the form of a Group discussion. It forms a major step in cases of MBAs, banks, administrative services, SSB, and in the marketing divisions of engineering companies. Again, very few students give any importance to this activity. They think that they would clear the GD rounds as they are smart, talented, and of course intelligent. After all, that is what has been told to them by their parents, teachers, and anybody who is externally interested in them. The candidates would be better equipped if they read the following few pages.

<u>Group Discussion.</u>

So much has been discussed about this topic of "group discussion" that when you read the title you most likely would have a wry smile on your face. I can already see that resigned look, which says "**Oh! Not again"** As a student aspiring for a job or as a professional seeking a better opportunity, we have all been subjected to a huge dose of **"Dos and Don'ts"** with respect to this GD aspect of the interview process. Also, it is the second favorite topic of ordinary trainers after the CV. There are books, articles, lectures, seminars, and workshops which tell us about how to approach GD. The current phrase is "cracking the GD" and almost all those who matter and also those who do not, are full of advice to all of us. Do they tell anything that can be claimed as a new input? I seriously have my doubts. Very rarely GDs serve the real purpose for which they were designed.

The process of GD is not new. Ever since there was a semblance of scientific management training people have been talking about the GD. I have my own share of GDs as a candidate, evaluator and now as a trainer. How does it help? A great deal if you may allow me to say so. I can say that I have an extended view spanning over three decades. So, in this essay, I would try to tell you, my view.

The first thing that strikes me when I think about GD is one simple rule. **The rule saysthat there is no thumb rule for GD**. I would always prepare myself for each GD on a case-to-case basis. What is good for one student may not be so in the case of another. Similarly, the criteria for one organization may not be acceptable to the other.

Secondly, the intensity with which the interviewing panel members approach the GD can be very vital.

- Are they energetic or tired?
- Do they really believe that the GD would give them the right candidates?
- Depending upon the quality of their previous experiences the members tend to attach significance to this whole activity.
- After all, they are doing their job like any other Indian. The personnel department people are undergoing the thrill or the torture of conducting the interviews, and as a result, they almost turn phlegmatic about the same.
- I always tend to sympathize (or is it empathize?) with the people in the personnel department for being exposed to candidates who are not up to the mark.
- It is not easy and I can imagine the strain, as the activity can many times turn monotonous.
- After all, I have been a GD evaluator myself and I can vouch for the stretching of the patience of the panelist by the candidates.

As the other half of the process, the candidates also have varying degrees of intensity and commitment. Very rarely, when both parties are equally interested in the GD, it can be a very satisfying experience and may serve the very purpose of conducting the GD. The purpose of the GD is simple. It acts as a filter with a big-size mesh. When the number of prospective candidates is much more than the expectations of the organization then the GD can be of great help, in form of a primary elimination round. Interaction with the more placeable candidates is welcome and the GD ensures this to an extent.

I have seen the candidates trying to dominate the group with the help of a loud voice, and /or more animation. One of my good friends sums it up very aptly. He says that such people are confident but their confidence is hollow. What can be more boring than a person who talks only with his voice rather than thoughts? Shouting is the first sign of shallowness, a lack of required knowledge and relevant information.

Parroting:

Due to peculiar teaching methods prevalent in our country, the candidates are not encouraged to read even the prescribed textbooks. The question sets culture has really spoilt the reading habits of the younger generation. Original thoughts or expressions from the candidates are usually scoffed at by the teachers. They prefer stereo-type Xerox answers. It gives a good-looking mark sheet to the candidates however the internalization of the subject is arguably overlooked. The candidates are either unaware of the correct procedures for the interviews and the GDs or they are confused because of the incorrect inputs received from incapable persons who claim to be the experts without any verifiable credentials.

Assertion and Aggression:

The candidates are required to understand the difference between assertion and aggression. The difference is a thin line that acts as a dividing line between success and failure. When a student states something with sound logic and facts and figures, in an acceptable tone, he is having a better chance to clear the GD. Aggression is mere sound, louder tone, and statements without any reasonable backup, hence more repulsive. So, the candidates must practice seriously what to say and more importantly how to say it. While he may not agree with everything that others say, he has to ensure that during the argument he should not confront others. The acceptable approach is conciliatory, not condescending.

Comprehension: Most candidates talk in the GD as if it is a burden on them. They give a distinct impression, that they are not ready to face the world, much less the corporate variety. Whether they have knowledge or not is again debatable but it is certain that they lack the approach. **Why should anybody else listen to you is the pertinentquestion**. Everyone has to answer for himself, and find ways to make his participation that much more interesting and meaningful.

What you speak at the GD is not only the current information but most of the time it has to be a **print-out of all that you have learned, read, and done in the tenure of the course**. Whether you were seriously reading the Business papers and /or the journals can be easily verified by the judges. The required level of language and the phrases which are relevant are conspicuous by their absence. So, the key phrase is one who reads leads in the GD.

Overall impact: The most important aspect about the student which finally tilts the scale in his favour is the overall impact he is able to create. Does he come across as a person whom the company would like to have on its team? It is not easy to decide on any readymade composition for a favourable impact and that is what makes it interesting.

There are certain suggestions that may be useful. The overall impact due to your persona takes a long time to build but gets tested and evaluated in less than a minute by the GD evaluators. Moreover, it is always with respect to the candidates who are almost similar to you. They are similarly equipped, taught, and trained by the same resources, so, it becomes a matter of personal charisma rather than anything else.

Before a candidate approaches the GD, he may read the following as a reminder.

Power of expression Ability to say clearly, correctly, and with content.

Knowledge of the subject the thought process and the range of the Thoughts

Liveliness Is he interested in what he is saying? Keenness & urge

Confidence outside and inside

The extent of participation Ability to influence the group, multiple strikes, at the mike

Flexibility Not single-tracked,

Disposition Cheerful and attentive

Accuracy In statements and data

Diction Others must understand what he says.

Practice Is he at ease or conscious of the Surrounding

Table manners No cross talks, no unwanted gestures.

Listening ability Can he list and enumerate what he listens

***

There are many candidates who behave very nicely till the time the results are announced. As soon as they find that their names do not figure in the selected list, they are a changed lot. All their manners are forgotten and they abuse each and every one. Many organizations are very smart. They do observe the candidates even at this stage and I know that candidates have been selected for their *mature* behavior, even when they were not cleared in the earlier evaluation. So have patience and remain on your best behavior till the time you are on the premises.

Even if you are not selected, please remember that **it is not the end of the world**. There are many more companies and jobs on offer. **So, keep on practicing and your time would soon come.**

4. PI: PERSONAL INTERVIEW The stage of a personal interview is extremely important as by this time you have almost cleared the tedious parts of the placement process. You have cleared the AT and GD. As per our calculation, you have cleared about 70% of the process. Now what remains between you and your placement is talking about **your**self, **your** aspirations, **your** objectives, **your** projects, **your** paper presentations, **your** participation in the various college or state activities, **your** domain knowledge, **your** family, and a few other things about you. If you are smart enough you would have noticed the repeated word... *your...*. What should be absolutely very easy if you know yourself and that you have practiced talking about yourself in an acceptable way? It is a simple assumption that you know yourself the best. How often do we see people fumble in this simple task? The reasons being

- Casual attitude: Students never talk about themselves just before the actual process of placement starts. A simple exercise of talking about self is very difficult. If you do not agree, try right now for the **next three minutes talking about yourself** and you would know what we mean.
- Absence of script: In the days of Net, SMS, WhatsApp, and FB people find it extremely difficult to actually write anything. So, it is suggested that before you appear for the placement process prepare a script for yourself and get it corrected and approved by the TPO. Your CV is not your **script** but it can help.
- Lack of practice: Even if you have the script ready you would be still far below par when you actually deliver the same.The ease is missing. Fluency is absent. The sequence is mixed up. When you have rehearsed in a proper way you would find that you appear natural and acceptable.

The candidates have to accept that special preparation is required for clearing personal interviews. In the case of campus interviews, the process is relatively simple compared to the interviews for administrative services, etc. The interview is a tool to recheck and re-establish the credibility of the candidate. So, there is a set pattern and most interviewers follow the same, without even realizing the same.

Also, the candidates have to understand that no person can understand the other person in such a short span of time. So, the process depends upon the averages, precedents, earlier experiences, and even earlier failed experiments. The impressions and the prejudices also affect the process.

The interview is a simple process and so keep it simple.

Interview simplified!

One of the most discussed topics across the globe is 'Job Interviews.' One who appears and the other who takes the interview have their viewpoints and they are rarely shy to discuss the same. A lot of reading and self-help material is available which can be used by job aspirants. Yet when you actually get in the interview room you suddenly find that you are very lonely, nervous, and most likely stressed. You also feel very cold which is not only because of the AC. You also find that you are in a vacuum of intellectual inertia. What you certainly knew before you entered the room has suddenly deserted you and you feel that you are sure to look and sound like a fool.

If you feel so, please be sure that you are in a majority.

Very few working people today can say something worthwhile about their interviews with some pride. They would tell you that given another chance they would have done better rather than what they actually did.

Let us try and understand the whole process in a very simple way.

Would it help you to clear the interview? .... Maybe!

In and Out:

Whatever little experience I have about attending, giving, and taking interviews tells me that it is a very simple process if you keep it simple. There is only one fact. **Either you are "In" or "Out."** There is no ATKT, grace marks, condos, and generally no second chances.

If you are **'in'** you are so-called salvaged. And if you are **'out'** please be sure to know that there would be always another chance. But the chance would help you only if **you change for the better** in between the two chances. If you keep on repeating the same approach and mistakes which has so far failed then very rarely you would produce a different result.

- So, are you ready to change?
- Are you ready to stretch?
- Are you ready to once again study?
- Are you ready to go back to basics?
- Are you ready to adapt to what **they (as recruiters)** want rather than what **you** think you have?

Interview simplified!

Please understand that in a short span of 15 to 20 minutes the interviewer would be mainly concentrating on finding out whether you fit in the general picture of the job profile. And he cannot check everything about you. He also depends upon certain thumb rules. There is something called as law of averages, the region you belong to, the previous experiences about your colleges, and the performances of your worthy seniors, contribute to your success. The image of the Institute is the single largest factor that contributes to the campus selection of students when everything else remains the same.

Time Division:

In any standard interview, the time divisions are very important. The first two minutes are extremely vital as they can give a clue to the interviewer about what you are and whether you are interesting enough for the interviewer, to proceed further.

The next part is generally about your education, to be closely followed by your projects. You have by now consumed about 10 to 12 minutes. If the interviewer wishes he may ask you about your hobbies, and extracurricular activities. The final impression is formed by the questions on the subject knowledge and in what way and language you are answering the same.

Projects:

Most professional students present a very light-hearted approach to the projects they submit for their degrees. They regret their mistake for the whole of remaining working life. The project is the nearest thing to actually working in the company, hence carries a lot of weight in the selection process. If you have actually done something serious it generally reflects on your face. It helps to prepare the project part very very seriously. The readymade projects sold in the market only benefit the ones who sell them to vulnerable students. They kill the ingenuity in the minds of the students. The devaluation of the process of working on a project, learning firsthand, overcoming the small and big problems, and demeaning of the truth is a few things that need to be understood. The student does not value such projects because he has not actually worked on the same.

The last things:

- By now the panelist is on the verge of deciding whether you are in or out. The last thing checked is about your fixations, prejudices, attitudes, and attributes.
- Are you rigid or flexible?

- Are you able to listen?
- What is your temper?
- Would you work unconditionally?
- Would you be in the blame mould?
- Are you satisfied with the salary component?
- Would you work in shifts?
- Would you work in a junior supervisory cadre?
- Would you work under a female boss?
- Are you aware of continuous evaluation?
- Would you work in interior towns?

There is a number of attitude check questions that need some in-depth analysis before you can answer them in the correct way. The process of the interview is linked with each component in a sort of treasure hunt. Unless you clear one step you are not allowed in the next. One mistake in one clue and you are out of the hunt.

Ready for rejection:

After you do everything right you may feel that you are bound to be selected. It is not so! You may still be rejected. Why? Because there are others who might have performed better! Or there might be illogical things that cause your downfall. Be prepared for all such eventualities. The good thing is that even today at least in the private sector good sense generally prevails and that reflects in the selections.

Common Ground:

You have understood that in this process of 15 to 20 minutes which decides your future you are supposed to speak about yourselves for the better part of the interview. What you have done, what are your achievements, why you selected your branch, what are your hobbies, and what is your family background are a few things you are supposed to talk about? Nobody can challenge your statements unless they are foolish. So, the only common ground is your knowledge about domain subjects. You are expected to know about and the interviewer generally knows better than you. So, he is in a position to evaluate whether you have done anything worthwhile in the tenure of your degree. It is not how you parrot but how you explain generally helps. Comprehension rather than reproduction is valued.

In a process where you have to deal most of the time with yourself and your skills and knowledge, how can you explain your fear and failure?

Whatever happens, you are supposed to know at least yourself. You should not and cannot fail if you take some basic steps and counsel yourself regularly.

Now that you have understood that interview is **a simple process** and there is no need to be afraid of appearing for an interview one more thing you need to understand is that the interview is a matter of appearance. There is no technique even today that can read your mind correctly. Let us understand appearance.

Interview: A matter of appearance.

Most of us have to clear some kind of interview for getting something worthwhile in our lives. Whether it is a job, a loan, or even a life partner, we have to face an interview. We put a heavy stake on the span of 15 or 20 minutes which may decide what we get or do not.

But in spite of being aware of the fact above, most of us do not actually prepare for the event and suffer very heavily. We feel that we might be the "lucky ones" who would get what we want without any preparation. **That never happens.** And if somebody is born lucky, even if gets what he wants, he is certain to make a complete mess of it before long.

Job interview, we know is a matter of half an hour at the most and yet affects a large part of our future existence. Why can't we prepare for the time? Why can't we pose and act? Why can't we make long-lasting impressions? Is it a matter of our communication, CV, experience, or anything else about which we still do not know? Why someone gets a job and the other does not? Is it a fair chance or something else?

Selection is more a function of appearance than the actual content of the candidates. **Is it?** Appearance is what you appear to others rather than what you think you are. There are certain safe thumb rules for creating a proper appearance that can produce surprising results.

Let us see these and understand them.

1. **Appear Decent**

Appearance is what we are and how we present ourselves. We cannot much change about how we look but we can certainly appear to have taken some care to improve the same. We can wear acceptable clothes, and attire and should not antagonize the person sitting in front. We should wear formal as far as possible. If your college has a regular uniform it helps to wear the same. Each body has its plusses. We also have. Such as height, features, hair, physique, and eyes. Are we using each to create a positive effect? The use of scent is very risky. Your entry should not be announced by your smell. The offensive hair oil, deodorants, and dabs of perfumes must be avoided.

The language your body speaks is more eloquent than words. In fact, most times you are either **in or out** evenbefore you speak a single word. Your walk before your talk is always very critically observed. So be careful about how you walk. Your body can also tell whether you are lazy, laidback, casual, sincere, attentive, angry, rebellious, amicable, a loner and so many other things, so be very careful about your body and what it tells others. A plain mirror can be a very good friend telling you the plain truths. The good thing about a body is that you can train it to yield proper results.

2. **Appear Sincere.**

A sincere person with a lower IQ has more chance of clearing an interview than a person who is intelligent but does not appear sincere. It is a known fact that employers do not prefer intelligent people. Their retention is the problem. You would appear sincere if you reach on time, well dressed and well groomed, with all relevant documents and while you wait, wait like a person who needs the job. Interact with the reception with some courtesy.

3. **Appear Intelligent:**

Appearing intelligent if possible is a slightly cynical way of putting it, but please recall the title of the essay and you would be ok. How does one appear intelligent? Is there a way? What is the accepted way of intelligent behavior? Let us see.

a. Intelligent people would not be impulsive. They would take some time before they answer.
b. They would understand the question before answering.
c. They would not give opinions. They would speak with facts, and figures rather than what they think about the topic in question.
d. The statements would be authenticated. They know the source and dates.
e. They would know how to explain things to the panelists.

Most of the time it is not what you say but how you say matters.

4. <u>Appear Interested:</u>

The person who is interested in the surroundings, ambiance, and the people around and can adjust generally is more acceptable. Listen very carefully to what the panelists are talking. Answer with at least some enthusiasm.

5. <u>Appear needy</u>:

A person may be very smart, very talented, and very capable but appears to be 'not needy' and has a very remote chance of getting selected. If he gives an impression that he is not a settling type he does not get a nod. The need and the severity of the need generally result in getting the job. Employers want people who would stay in their jobs rather than flash.

6. <u>Appear Confident:</u>

What you may do to appear confident. Each one is nervous at the time of the interview, which is beside the point. What matters is how you can mask your nervousness. Please remember that confidence comes from practice. Have you rehearsed your act? How often? You can do it again and again till you are confident of clearing the interview.

As said earlier the interviewer has to stick to some basic rules which help him to decide on the candidate's selection. Whatever steps he does take, he has to take a chance. **Mostly he is more aware than anyone else of this fact**. It never hurts you if you <u>help him to decide in your favor</u>. If you want a decent job with a <u>decent</u> salary in a <u>decent</u> company with <u>a decent</u> designation you ensure that you win the game of a decent appearance.

So, the PI is a process that you can master to a great extent and clear it when it matters most for your career. One more important aspect that no trainer generally explains is as follows:

In a span of about fifteen to twenty minutes, the interviewer can ask a maximum of 10 questions. Each question answered properly, takes you closer to a salary of say Rs. 5 lakhs. So, each question is worth about Rs. 50,000/-. It pays to cross-check whether or not the answers given by you are worth the amount.

5. **HRPI: HUMAN RESOURCE PERSONAL INTERVIEW.**: The last and one of the most important steps is the HR interview in the campus placement process. By now you have cleared 95 % of the process either in a smooth or labored way, but what matters is that you are here in front of HR. You have to remind yourself that if you flunk the interview here, then you are the only person who is to be blamed. It hurts very badly and many students just break down into sobs if they are rejected at this stage.

The HR people are a smart variety of human beings and moreover, they are exposed to students like you day in and day out. So, before they decide to give you an all-important offer letter they would like to check and recheck the essential aspects and the relevant documents. Generally, the HR person is very pleasant and almost friendly. But behind this exterior, a very cold and calculating smart mind is scrutinizing you.

So, a few suggestions for you:

When seating in front of an HR person or a panel never be over-smart. Answer all their questions with equal seriousness as you were in the PI. Generally, be pleasant, and accept his terms and conditions. Appear interested. Say yes to everything. Talk good about everything. College is good, specialization is good, your city, family, country, industry everything is good. Do not give opinions. Do not criticize anything. If you follow these lines, you are most likely to get the coveted offer letter.

All students are capable to get the job they want. They just do not have faith in their own potential. The lack of faith results in a lack of preparation. The TPO is the only person who can instill confidence and help the students to accomplish the goal of getting a placement.

So, all the very best!

***

CHAPTER XV

The DIGITALISATION (The world at the fingertips)

The Digitalisation

(The world at the fingertips)

Every process ideally needs to change in due course of time. The time of the change is the key factor for future success. The difference between sight and vision affects the way the process changes to adapt to the new incoming trends.

Training and placements activity is no exception. In the last few years, so many things have changed. The academic subjects, the specializations, the new techniques of teaching, the world order, the economics, and the Covid-19 endemic, but nothing has impacted the world the way digitalization has affected the world. *Nothing* is done the way it was done a few years back. *Online is the only thing that is in the line.* The online is hand in hand with the latest concept of artificial intelligence, AI. Had it not been for digitalization the world would have been at a standstill in the endemic time of two years and would have faced the greatest disaster.

The endemic Covid -19 forced the entire mankind to change the way we live, eat, think, communicate, work, and even respire. Nobody could imagine such a calamity, even in his wickedest nightmare. But it happened. Like all other fields, it affected education also. It changed the lives of many students for no fault of theirs. The students were forced to study at home which they wanted when they were tired of attending college. They realized the contribution of mixing with peers, peer learning, student teachers, and relationships while they were forced to sit in front of a non-living screen of a mobile or a tab. It affected even worse for the students in the final years of their course. They missed all learning that they would have otherwise acquired by simply attending college. The physical connect was missing.

The employment activity was at a standstill, and, so was the production in many units, throughout the world. The colleges were closed. Exams were postponed in worse cases canceled. There was chaos and every person was affected in some way or the other. It was a matter of mere survival so everything else took a backseat. That India could manage to come back is a tribute to many people and many processes which continued in the extreme conditions.

But there were some blessings in disguise due to the endemic. The new concept of *"work from home"* emerged. Education was less affected, as schools and colleges subsequently opted for online classes.

The companies especially the HR departments found that working in the virtual world helps them to deliver at a speed that was not earlier possible. With less staff and less traveling, the HRD can hire more numbers with relative ease and comfort. So, in the years to come corporate hiring would be more digital and they would expect that the institutes would be compatible with the new requirements of the hiring processes.

The T&P also had to adapt to this new trend. It has affected the way the campus drives were held. Earlier most drives were held physically on the campus or any other venue decided by either the college or the corporate. It was a physical activity involving a lot of planning resources and money. The time spent by the executives both on the supply and demand side was huge. The results were influenced by prejudices and choices. When the process is controlled by the software the same can be controlled at a single point and the students from the entire universe can participate provided the company wishes to allow it. The evaluation is almost instant and automatic. No human interface is really required. At the same time, the accuracy is much better.

However, the digital process somehow stops at the CV/ and aptitude test stage. CVs can be submitted online. The AT can be conducted online. The GD and PI still have to be conducted by human interaction. GD somehow would present some difficulty at least as of today, maybe at a later date, it would be conducted by using conference calls. Of course, the interview can be held online, but for a fresher, it would be better if he attends a physical interview. One thing is certain the volume of students for the GDPI is greatly reduced. Moreover, the sample for the GD and PI is already enriched, as well as positively filtered and hence there are more chances of selection hits per drive than the earlier versions of the campus drives.

The time frame would be changed. The traveling would be reduced. The desperation at the end of the physical drives is avoided. The unfair means are avoided.

There is so much information available and TPO would be tempted to get dragged by the magnetic force of available information. He can do so, nothing wrong with it, as long as he is doing it for his knowledge. What he has to understand is that his job of training and preparing the students (for the physical or virtual campus drives,) **remains almost unchanged.** His students would still have to submit a CV, clear the AT, participate, clear the GD, and finally have to pass the personal interview. The basics remain the same.

So, what is changing?

We have entered a digital era and because of this, the entire process has changed in the way we approach the campus drive. The data, its collection, its analysis, its transfer, and finally even the way the tests/ interviews. are conducted.

Recruitment or talent acquisition or in simple language hiring employees can be defined as the process of attracting, selecting, and hiring the right or optimally compatible person for the vacant position in the organization. The requirement is raised by the concerned department head and the more exact the job description in results in getting the more suitable person for the job. There is one more very important aspect which is the cost per acquisition of employees. The recruitment has to be the best but at the lowest possible cost. Digitalization has helped in cutting the costs of hiring. The travel is reduced, and the online interviews cost practically nothing so corporates are happily shifting their focus to the digital version of operations. It also breaks the geographical barriers as it does not matter whether the job aspirant is in Pune, Bangalore, or California.

The companies would have developed their customized systems to evaluate the candidates. The evaluation parameters would be different and maybe more analytical on a micro level. The analysis by software is faster and at times more accurate.

Digital strategy: The strategy is defined as a medium to long-term application of the best options available to optimize the objectives of the mission. The business strategies include planning, planning team, data procurement, and execution team. **One has to understand that all future business strategies would be digital strategies**. Any organization irrespective of the field of its operations would have to adapt to this latest dynamic change just to stay afloat. To be at the top of the business ladder they would have to be on their toes, and very alert to even the smallest change in the environment anywhere in the world.

So, for a TPO the digital strategy (read as the ultimate goal) is to place the maximum number of students in the best available companies, then how does he go about it?

As a **first step,** he has to align all his efforts with the requirements of the company. This means that he has to seek digital transformation in his college. For a sound digital strategy, he has to ensure that he has digitally transformed the working of the college, or at least his department, to begin with. He has to understand the difference between strategy and transformation. Strategy is more complex and comprehensive whereas the transformation is the early changes in the present-day setup. The transformation expects coordination across every department of the college and the changes in the behavior of the organization in the college. The strategy on the other hand has less attention on the behavior but involves technology. So, the decision of which strategy to be adopted is to be taken by the management and then adapt to the required technology to be able to compete with the best in business.

The second step is to understand that the placement activity has more to do with the commercial activity than the academics and run it like a business. The decisions are based on the cost of placement per student. If there mix up here the equation is disturbed and the results would not be as pleasant as they could have been.

The third step is about understanding the VUCA world and how to survive in the same. VUCA means vision, understanding, clarity, and agility together to enable the organization to survive and excel in the constantly changing and unpredictable economic and geopolitical world. The world now changes faster than it would a few decades ago. The TPO has to be aware and should be more than prepared to adapt so that his students are not caught napping. They should be ready to work in such dynamic situations and profitably use them. They should be resilient, and able to quickly learn and adapt.

In terms of a placement scene, the pre-recruitment tests, the data screening, the scheduling of virtual interviews, and career fairs would undergo a tremendous change. It would be faster and more AI-dependent. The TPO would be greatly helped if he studies the new CRT software. The newer versions of ATS and CRM need to be studied.

It is wise to remember that all the digitalization techniques are very good. They would change the facilitation techniques for the TPO. **But the basics would remain the same.** The core of a student would still be sincere, teachable, and strong in communication, and the rest of the things would revolve around the core. What is ideally desired in a digitally controlled environment is an *attitude, aptitude, technical competency, 360° approach,* *awareness beyond the textbooks, learning ability, flexibility, and communication ability* of the students.

In simple language, the TPO must be able to process the student data quickly despite disruptions. Disruption in the external and internal factors would require not just continuous evaluation, but along with continuous calibration of the valuation systems. The people working would be subjected to a ruthless appraisal, because in absence of the same the company would be in rough waters. If he continues to perform in situations well beyond his control his students would learn the importance of being flexible, teachable, and professionally competent. The system may work superbly, but does it work in a similar way when under stress is what new generation managers have to work. Working with a clear mind and correctly would lead the students to a bright future.

***

Conclusion

Conclusion

The training for placement activity is simple if we keep it simple. It is well documented, and done nationally and internationally, year after year with various degrees of success. That there is no winning formula even today, tells us that there are many grey areas, which people do not want to see or if they do at all see, they just want to overlook. The basic conflict of interest is very obvious, which makes it very difficult for this department, and the disinterest is never subtle. The range of colleges is widespread, where on one hand, they claim hundred percent placements, or on the other, those colleges that celebrate even a single placement, both, use more or less the same process. At least as of today, the basic process remains the same.

The steps in the process are CV/AT/GD/ PI/HRPI.

What is the main reason that changes the outcome is the approach of the students and the TPO and his responses to the changing situations and environment around him in a constant fashion.

Students: All students irrespective of their category like A+ /A /B/ Or C face a few problems when they go through the process of placements. The students from premier institutes have their issues with expectations and the students from no so good institutes have their own set of problems. The premier students may not face operational problems but they do have issues with the company, payment packages, job profiles, and future in the company. The premier students have problems of plenty. They are difficult to be trained, because of their intelligence, attitude, and very high expectations. It is well-known fact that the attitude word has a hidden negative shade.

The average students have a different set of problems. Their problems are mainly due to a perceived inability and improper focus. They feel the effects of their teacher's and parent's usual rhetoric that they are not up to requisite standards. The initial effort to at least try what the TPO is telling them proves to be their tallest hurdle. They also feel a fear of failure. That they can succeed with whatever they have as qualities are the only aspect the TPO has to transfer and they pick up the speed. The language, the domain knowledge, the soft skills, and the smile can all be learned if their attitude aspect is fine-tuned, students can surprise a few and most importantly themselves.

The TPO has to base all his activities on the following:

1. His process is good and it can deliver the required results. His belief level is the most important driving force which sees him through the hurdles posed by the students, staff, teachers, parents, and companies.
2. The students are good. They want to improve. They would win the final lap.
3. Skillsets required for the placements can be imparted and learned by the students.
4. The students do not need the full dose of personality development. Excessive training can prove repulsive. More information imparted to the student makes him feel that he would have to prepare very hard for the placements. *This is against the principles of training.* Trainer thrives on the promise of *learning small things* for achieving what the students want. The TPO has to check, diagnose and then customize the extent of refinement and training for each student against what he had said as his placement requirement. The goalpost was then decided and later should not be changed.
5. Like all other processes in our lives, the process of placements would not be received by all students. The ratio of those who respond and those who ignore is different in each institute, each batch, and each season of placements. So far as it is below the danger mark the TPO should carry on his work of identifying the training needs, polishing, and encouraging the students.
6. The students immediately identify fake sympathy and false promises. So, the TPO must restrain from overselling.
7. When the students deviate from the training requirements the TPO must remember that even the best team of trainers and trainees faced this problem. After the best training effort for over fifty years, concluded by one of the best sessions in human life and motivation, after solving all queries, the best trainer Yogeshwar Shrikrishna must **have been amazed** by the stupid behavior of Arjun when Abhimanyu was killed in the war. So, the TPO should have a strong option for mid-course correction.
8. He has to surrender to the fact that he is a nonplaying captain. He has to patiently watch the success and failure of his students.
9. The TPO has to understand that if the placements are good, the credit would be given to all like the principal, staff, and professors. The TPO

has to be gracious enough and accept.

10. No two seasons of placements can be similar. So, the overall process of placements remains the same but the TPO has to look for the variation and finetune the system continuously.
11. The TPO has to be aware of the global trends and he should be able to apply them to his students.

So, to conclude the TPO must remember that no problem is bigger than the solution. He may also remember that the solution can be evasive but it is there.

He has to work on adopting a missionary attitude and hoping for the best. He should not forget that he is doing a thankless job and never vie for credit for the success in the process.

***

www.ingramcontent.com/pod-product-compliance
Ingram Content Group UK Ltd.
Pitfield, Milton Keynes, MK11 3LW, UK
UKHW021914190726
13853UKWH00002B/669